CHARLES HANDY

BEYOND CERTAINTY

The Changing Worlds of Organisations

ARROW
BUSINESS BOOKS

Arrow Books Limited 1996

1 3 5 7 9 10 8 6 4 2

© Charles Handy 1995, 1996

The right of Charles Handy to be identified as the author
of this work has been asserted by him in accordance
with the Copyright, Designs and Patents Act, 1988.

Arrow Books Limited
20 Vauxhall Bridge Road, London SW1V 2SA

Random House Australia (Pty) Limited
16 Dalmore Drive, Scoresby, Victoria 3179, Australia

Random House New Zealand Limited
18 Poland Road, Glenfield
Auckland 10, New Zealand

Random House South Africa (Pty) Limited
PO Box 2263, Rosebank 2121, South Africa

RANDOM HOUSE UK Limited Reg. No. 954009

Papers used by Random House UK Limited
are natural, recyclable products made from wood grown in
sustainable forests. The manufacturing processes conform to
the environmental regulations of the country of origin

Companies, institutions and other organizations wishing to make bulk
purchases of any business books published by Random House should
contact their local bookstore or Random House direct:
Special Sales Director
Random House
20 Vauxhall Bridge Road
London SW1V 2SA
Tel: 0171 973 9670 Fax: 0171 828 6681

Printed and bound in Great Britain by
Cox & Wyman Ltd, Reading, Berkshire

ISBN 0 09 954991 3

BEYOND CERTAINTY

Charles Handy is a writer and broadcaster, known to many for his 'Thoughts for Today' on the BBC's *Today* programme. He was named as Business Columnist of the Year in 1994 for some of his pieces in this collection. His books, including *The Empty Raincoat*, have sold over one million copies worldwide. He has been, in his time, an oil executive, a business economist, a Professor at the London Business School and Chairman of the Royal Society of Arts. He and his wife Elizabeth, a portrait photographer, live in London, Norfolk and Tuscany.

CONTENTS

◆

ACKNOWLEDGEMENTS

◆

The author and publishers are grateful to the following for permission to reproduce the essays in this collection:

Harvard Business School Press, for 'Beyond Certainty' (copyright © 1994 by the President and Fellows of Harvard College)
Lear's magazine, for 'The Coming Work Culture'
Harvard Business Review, for 'Balancing Corporate Power: A New Federalist Paper (copyright © 1992 by the President and Fellows of Harvard College)
RSA Journal, for 'What is a Company For?'
Director magazine, for 'Are Jobs For Life Killing Enterprise?' and all subsequent essays

INTRODUCTION

◆

THE CLOUDS ON THE HORIZON

Adam Smith, the high priest of market economies and of
modern capitalism, may well be the most quoted and least
read of all authors. Who, for instance, knows that he wrote
this:

> A profitable speculation is presented as a public good
> because growth will stimulate demand, and everywhere
> diffuse comfort and improvement. No patriot or man of
> feeling could therefore oppose it. [But] the nature of this
> growth, in opposition, for example, to older ideas such as
> cultivation, is that it is at once undirected and infinitely
> self-generating in the endless demand for all the useless
> things in the world.

Adam Smith, you should be alive today, to take a walk
through the shopping malls or the tourist streets of our cities.
You would see windows stacked high with trivia, with all the
detritus of a throwaway society, where growth depends on
persuading more and more people to buy more and more
things that they may want but can hardly need. Yet, without
that induced demand, there wouldn't be the growth which
would spread Adam Smith's 'comfort and improvement' to
those who really need it. We need our economies of glitz and
sleaze to provide work of a sort for many of our people.

'Work of a sort' is, indeed, all that much of it can ever be. The best management in the world can't make meaningful work out of stacking shelves or packing boxes, or out of selling T-shirts, mugs or plastic toys, or even plastic food. This is toil and drudgery, not the decent work we demand as the right of all. It is toil done for money, the money which alone provides access to the rich economy we have promised ourselves.

It is a strange irony, just one of many which itch away at our modern state. To give our people the necessities of modern life we have to spend more of our money and more of their time on the non-necessities, on the 'useless things', the junk of life. Worse – to produce these things we consume the world's resources, pollute its environment, muck up its countryside and dirty its towns and cities. This was not the brave new world that capitalism promised with its freedom of choice in the markets of the world.

We thought, once, that we could have it all, that money could buy us choice in everything, and technology would deliver it. If we wanted no children, then technology would allow us the joys of mating without the consequences, and if later we changed our minds, technology could put that right, too. Death could be postponed, if not indefinitely, at least for a decade or so, and society would make sure that the old did not clutter up the lives of their children by making the state responsible for their wellbeing. The state, in fact, would take care of everything we did not want to do for ourselves. The Basic German Law, for example, lists 17 basic individual rights but not one individual duty except to pay taxes, sometimes. Unlimited economic growth, in short, would provide the wherewithal for all our wants, and technology would somehow deal with any unwanted consequences.

CHARLES HANDY

It was always an unlikely dream. There are always unintended consequences to rational policies. The understandable attempt, in China, to ration children to one per family is producing a generation of 'child emperors', only sons, spoilt rotten, the daughters too often aborted. The American freedom to live where you choose, and to choose whom you live with, in that vast country, results in ghettoes of the rich, ghettoes of the old and, inevitably, ghettoes of the underclass. Community as an ideal turns into a selfish exclusivity, reminiscent of the city-states of medieval Europe – great for those inside, but tough for the outsiders, which is why the insiders built high walls around themselves.

And when we finally confront some of the costs of our extravagances in the First World, and ask the Third World of developing countries to do things differently lest we destroy our firmament, they, not unnaturally, want some of those extravagances for themselves before they make the sacrifices which we ask for. We are caught in a trap of our own devising, unwilling to accept that freedom of choice can't easily be rationed. How nice it would be, I sometimes think, when crushed in a tourist mob in Florence or Seville, if only a fortunate few (including myself, naturally) had the means and the choice to travel. Freedom of choice for all can easily create misery for most.

Organizations have not been immune to the lure of false promises. Good jobs for all, well-paid jobs, was one of those promises. As a result, more and more people, particularly women, wanted those jobs. But organizations also needed to be efficient, and that meant doing the same, or, if possible, more, with fewer people. In the last 25 years Europe's economy grew by 70%, but only 10% new jobs were created, not nearly enough for all those that wanted them. The faster we grow, it begins to seem, the fewer people we need to work our organizations.

Our people are now our assets, proclaim those same organizations, offering the promise of a caring, nurturing community at work; a Japanese tradition translated to Western ways. But assets, it turned out, were things to be milked as well as nurtured, and those lucky enough to have one of those proper jobs inside the organization found themselves working ever harder and longer, squeezing the traditional 100,000 hours of a working life into 30 years instead of 50. That works out at 67 hours a week, leaving little time for families, or for anything else, come to that. Organizations are rightly seen as the instruments of wealth creation, whether the wealth be money, health, education or service of one type or another, but we now see more clearly that, in their turn, the individuals inside the organization have become *its* instruments, subordinated to the goals of the organization, used and/or discarded as needed. This was not intended.

Nor was it intended that the brilliant invention of limited liability would end up with companies 'owned' by people who had never been near them, let alone met with their people or devised their products and their strategies. Companies as pieces of property, to be bought and sold by speculators, makes money the measure of all things and shortens the time-horizons of all those involved.

Many other things were not intended. It was not intended that women should be squeezed out of the new, efficient organizations. A more liberal age wanted it quite otherwise, but those 67-hour weeks meant that too often it had to be a choice between job or children. We must hope that many women will, in future, choose children, or find some better way to combine the two, because the birthrate in most affluent societies is now less than 1.5 children per woman. Too many children may be China's problem, but too few children is little better – a society of greying elders with ever fewer people to support them, and no way, this time, that technology can change things inside of 50 years. We shall all be worse off than our fathers and mothers were, a state which many Americans already are shocked to find themselves in today.

THERE IS BETTER NEWS

It is now clear that economic growth for all forever is not on the cards. Even if it were, it would be no guarantee of happiness. In the last 20 years the British economy grew by 40%, the German by 50% and the Japanese by 60%, but it is by no means obvious that the Germans and the Japanese are any happier. In fact, surveys show the reverse, with the Japanese envious of the lifestyles of almost everyone. Perhaps we will soon cease to pursue the chimera of everlasting economic growth and harken to Adam Smith's reminder of 'cultivation' as a primary goal.

If we do, it will be more from the force of circumstance than from choice, but events shape values as much as values shape events, and the events which are coming up will confront us all with new choices. In the past, most of us were seemingly content to sell all our working time to the organization, to do with it what they willed, within reason. Our choices were mainly to do with how we spent the money they gave us and the time which they left us. Not unnaturally, money dominated our values, and the things that money might be able to buy. The more money the more choice. It was, inevitably, for most people, a materialistic world.

It was also an institutional world. Most people got their sustenance and their structure from organizations of one sort or another. Those organizations resonated with power, authority and control. We may not always have liked what they said or what they required of us, but it was clear where authority resided. That is about to change.

Our world is about to see a change as significant as the technological event which, in many ways, launched Europe into a new age 600 years ago when the printing press was invented and developed. For the first time, then, people were able to read the Bible in their own language in their own home in their own time. No longer did they have to go to church to hear the word of God, in Latin, interpreted by a licensed minister of the Church. They could now make up their own minds about right and wrong, God and the devil. As a result, the authority of the Church crumbled, and with it the authority of most institutions. Individual freedom led to creativity, which blossomed into the Renaissance; but this freedom also produced schisms and anarchy, conflict and repression as people everywhere sought to flex their muscles and to take charge of their own destiny. Others, naturally, yearned for the days of order and discipline and, where they could, tried to restore them.

The television set and the telephone, with the computer at the end of it, the wired and unwired world which we now contemplate, are the modern equivalents of the printing press. When Motorola achieves its dream of a personal telephone for everyone with a personal number for each of us at birth, then a telephone will truly belong to a person not a place. Insignificant as that sounds, it means that the office will become as unnecessary as the churches became. Television already allows each of us to make up our own minds about the affairs of the world, eroding the mystique of presidents, prime ministers, queens and corporate chairmen. CD-Roms and the Internet make the knowledge of the world available to all, depriving teachers everywhere of their competitive advantage over their students, authority eroded there as well.

As in the Renaissance, it will be an exciting time, a time of great opportunities for those who can see and seize them, but of great threat and fear for many. It will be more difficult to hold organizations and societies together. The softer words of leadership and vision and common purpose will replace the tougher words of control and authority because the tough words won't bite any more. Organizations will have to become communities rather than properties, with members not employees, because few will be content to be owned by others. Societies will break down into smaller units but will also regroup into even larger ones than now for particular purposes. Federalism, an old doctrine, will become fashionable once again, in spite of its inherent contradictions.

Interestingly, many of the products of this new wired age will be less destructive of our environment. CD-Roms consume no trees. The new economic growth areas of health, education, personal services and leisure activity need far fewer raw materials and are more to do with psychological and physical enrichment than with 'things'. These new growth areas also come in smaller, more people-friendly organizations than the manufacturing giants of the past. 'Things' will be increasingly made by 'things' anyway, and not by human automatons. As society ages, more people will have enough of things, mostly, and will be in the slimming-down stage of life. They may, in fact, be more interested in Adam Smith's 'cultivation' than in 'useless things', and if cultivation is marketable we shall have economic growth as well.

We may discover that when we can, increasingly, choose how to spend our time, it may not always make sense to sell it as expensively as we can or as much of it as we can. There are other things which we can do with time, even if it is only to sit and talk with friends. Many will use their time to increase their skills and enlarge their range of talents because intelligence is now the pathway to wealth and power. Time and talent will become the commodities in most demand, and they will be the property of each individual, not of the corporation, changing the balance of power quite radically. Education will, once again, become a prized and precious thing, at all ages and of all types.

The danger, of course, is that this 'cultivation' becomes a reality only for the privileged few in the privileged world of the rich countries. We shall have to take on board the truth that you don't make the poor rich by making the rich richer and hoping that the riches will trickle down, because they don't. Paradoxically, it works the other way round – you make the rich richer by making the poor rich, because then they have more money to spend. To start the cycle, however, you first have to invest in the poor, enlarging their capabilities, enhancing their skills, underwriting their initiatives. This works for the world at large as well as for individual societies, and even for organizations, but it always calls for short-term sacrifice by the rich in the beginning.

Sacrifices, however, are only made, voluntarily, for goals and ideals we believe in, and when we have confidence in those who may lead us there. Leadership, therefore, becomes more important than ever in this new world, and philosophy, or the search for the meaning of things, becomes the driving force of economics. Individually, we shall each of us be more responsible for our own destiny, with no organizations there to run our lives for us, and that will force us to be clear about our own priorities in life. Circumstances will, therefore, make philosophers of us all.

THE LOGIC OF THIS BOOK

The essays in this book reflect my concerns with this world we are entering. An essay is, literally, an attempt or a test, a stab at the answer. My essays and speeches are exactly that – a sighting shot at the truth. They are, for me, therefore, the raw material of my other writings. Sometimes the raw material makes for more interesting reading than the finished book, being more tentative and more of the moment. It also comes in bite-sized bits which, for busy people, can make it more digestible.

The essays in this book cover the last five years. They contain the seeds of what were to be two books in that time – *The Age of Unreason* and *The Empty Raincoat* – but there is much else besides, depending on the context of the times and the particular audience to whom they were addressed. Putting what I think are the better essays together in a book resurrects them from the files and allows me to share them with a wider group than their first audiences. Like all collections of this sort, however, it is a book to dip into, rather than to read through at a sitting.

The common strand of all the essays is Uncertainty. Two and a half thousand years ago, Heraclitus reminded his listeners that you could never step into the same river twice – it was forever changing, as was life. We have never wanted to believe him. In the first of these essays – 'Beyond Certainty: A Personal Odyssey' – I explain how I myself came to realize that there was no certainty any more in human things, and how a search for point and meaning had to move up our agendas if we were not to be caught hanging around waiting for some mythical leader to tell us where to go and how to get there.

The next three essays deal with what have been, for me, the most important building blocks in my thinking about how the world of work and business can best develop. The first, 'The Coming Work Culture', was written to introduce the idea of 'portfolio' working to an American public. It was written for *Lear's*, a magazine for the new generation of working women. It reflects my feeling that work is getting more fragmented, that the independents would be a key feature of the new workplace and, most importantly, that this signalled a new opportunity for women.

The second, 'Balancing Corporate Power: A New Federalist Paper', written for the *Harvard Business Review*, explores what seems to be happening to the organization as it tries to be all things to all people, big but small, global but local, specialist but general. The title is meant to suggest that we can sometimes find the clues to the future in ideas from the past. Federalism has been around, as a concept, for 2,000 or more years, but we seem to have forgotten, both in politics and in business, what its key principles really are, as spelt out by, among others, the writers of the Federalist Papers in early America. This essay was awarded the McKinsey Award for the best article that year in the *Review*.

The third of these three core essays, 'What is a Company For?', was a speech delivered to a gathering at the Royal Society for the Encouragement of Arts, Manufactures and

Commerce, in London, in memory of Michael Shanks, one of Britain's stirrers and shakers in the early 1980s. In it, I challenge whether the conventional view of the company, as a piece of property owned by the shareholders, is a viable concept as we move into a more interwoven society, one where shareholders are not so much owners as investors. Who, then, are the real trustees of the future of our corporate wealth? This paper later stimulated an important enquiry by the Society into Tomorrow's Company, its role and responsibilities in our society.

Looking again at these papers, there is nothing which I regret saying and, apart from some minor updating of the figures, nothing which I want to change. The world is still unfolding as I suspected it would, and the discomforts are as great, but the changes too little. I remain optimistic about the possibilities of the future but pessimistic about our willingness to seize them.

There then follow 31 shorter pieces from the *Director* magazine, the journal of Britain's Institute of Directors. Once every two months, for the last five years, the editor of this journal, Stuart Rock, and his colleagues, have allowed and encouraged me to sound off on any subject which I would like to bring to the notice of their readers, the senior managers and directors of Britain's businesses. I have left these essays unabridged and in chronological order because they offer a sort of diary of my preoccupations of the moment.

Having said that, I have been startled to realize that my 31 preoccupations are still valid, now. Things, surprisingly, have not changed that much. We are not, as I see it, doing very much to influence our destinies, either as a country, as businesses, or, indeed, as individuals. None of these essays seems dated except, in one or two instances, in their introductions where my thoughts were triggered by a particular event. That is depressing. Life can still be a self-fulfilling prophecy even if we do nothing.

Britain, like most of Europe, is a prisoner of her history, which is long and, occasionally, glorious. Because the history is long we feel that the future, too, will be a long time in coming. We may be surprised. The premise behind all these essays is that we don't have to wait for that future; we can shape it, but there isn't much time. It would be sad if we missed our future because of our past.

ONE

◆

BEYOND CERTAINTY: A PERSONAL ODYSSEY

These last ten years have changed a lot of things. Ten years ago we thought that we knew where we stood, where we wanted to get to and how to get there. Internationally, the aim of the Western world was to ward off the threat of communism, both militarily and economically. Nationally, we were at the height of the Reagan/Thatcher years, more meant better, and it seemed, then, that more of everything was on offer if we could only get the price and the quality right. Individually, greed was good, even if we talked more delicately of achievement and personal wealth creation. We knew how to run organizations, too, or thought that we did, and management tomes hit the best-seller lists for the first time, with their varied recipes for excellence. It was a time of certainty.

It was a heady time, in its way. Certainty has its seductions, and it was comforting to see that George Orwell had been wrong in his dismal forecast of 1984, in his book of that name, with its other form of certainty, of a Big Brother watching all and ordering all. As a sceptical Irishman I was dubious, at first, of such vainglorious confidence, but scepticism could not long survive the self-congratulatory colleagues with their tales of their killings in the markets, their soaring bonuses and house prices, or, in Britain, the surge of relieved pride in the recent Falklands victory, and the sense that the world was back where it should be with the right people winning. I even wrote a book called *Understanding Organizations*, suggesting that such places could be understood, and their doings predicted.

There seemed, for a time, to be no end to it. In the golden days of the summer of 1987 I succumbed to the lure of a soaring stock market and housing boom. A developer asked me what price I wanted for my apartment in a London suburb. We had paid £10,000 for it ten years before and loved it dearly, but in 1987 everything, even one's cherished home, had a price, so: 'One million pounds,' I told him. 'Done,' he said, and, aghast at my daring, I went into the kitchen to tell my astonished family that I was an instant millionaire. We instructed our respective lawyers to start drawing up contracts while my wife and I took off for Italy to celebrate twenty-five years of mostly happy marriage. There, flushed with confidence and the certainty, now, of material success, I bought her a Tuscan villa. Why not? What else would a millionaire academic give his wife in those times?

I should have known, of course, that there is a curvilinear logic in the universe, and that nothing lasts forever. The curve always turns downward in the end, but wise are they who know when the turn will come. Just for a time, however, we all thought that, in many ways, we had found the curve to defy gravity, that we had stumbled on the elusive Theory of Everything in human affairs, that we really would be able to replicate success in every field and bring prosperity, and, with it, peace to the whole world.

We came back to London from Italy on the first Thursday

in October. That night, on BBC television, the weather forecast noted a small hurricane brewing in the Bay of Biscay, off the French coast, but in those days even the weather forecasters were certain. 'Believe me,' the man said, 'there will be no hurricane here.' That night the South of England was hit by the worst storm in 200 years. Britain is not used to hurricanes and the damage was immense. London was blacked out – an omen, surely, for the following Monday. Black Monday, when stock markets collapsed all over the world.

Within days, my million-pound house sale collapsed. There was no money any longer for such dreams in a developer's eye. I now had an Italian villa which I did not need and could not afford. Thus had the illusion of certainty made a monkey of me. That, however, was only a trivial personal affair. More serious was the general unravelling of certainty. Everywhere, now, there was doubt, uncertainty and scepticism again. Even our traditional foes started to behave in untraditional ways. 'We have a secret weapon,' Gorbachev told Reagan once. 'We shall cease to be your enemy.' Indeed, the Pentagon, I was told, with all its plans for every Cold War contingency, had no plans for winning it.

At the same time, the greed of Boesky and others landed them in prison – something which had never featured in *their* plans – and, one by one, the examples of excellence in organizations stumbled and faltered. House owners discovered that equity could be negative, when their mortgages exceeded the falling prices of their homes, and the market for second-hand Porsches slumped in London, as many of the whizz-kids of the markets discovered that their starry careers had reached a sudden and unexpected end.

It was a confusing time, those middle years of this past ten years. There was some short-lived jubilation at the domino-like collapse of the communist regimes and at a Gulf War, but these turned out to be Pyrrhic victories, leaving more problems than they solved, problems which were now for the victors to worry about. Exultantly, we tried to introduce the philosophy of capitalism into the old communist world, certain that what had worked so well for us would work for them, but such certainty did not last long. Nor did the military certainty of the Gulf War seem to have much relevance for the next conflict, in the old Yugoslavia.

I wrote another book then, *The Age of Unreason*. Its central philosophical theme was that change was now, rather obviously, discontinuous; no longer was change a straight projection of past trends into the future. When change is discontinuous, I argued, the success stories of yesterday have little relevance to the problems of tomorrow; they might even be damaging. The world, at every level, has to be reinvented to some extent. Certainty is out, experiment is in. The future then belongs, said George Bernard Shaw, another Irishman, to the unreasonable ones, the ones who look forward not backward, who are certain only of uncertainty and who have the ability and the confidence to think completely differently. Everything *could* be different, I believed – organizations, careers, schools, societies – and many of them should be different, but the real lesson which we had to learn was a new way of approaching life.

When I went to school, I did not learn anything much which I now remember, except for this hidden message, that every major problem in life had already been solved. The trouble was that I did not yet know the answers. Those answers were in the teacher's head or in her textbook but not mine. The aim of education, in that world of certainty, was to transfer the answers from the teacher to me, by one means or another. It was a crippling assumption. For years afterwards, when confronted with a problem which was new to me, I ran for an expert. It never occurred to me, in that world of certainty, that some problems were new, or that I might come up with my own answers. I was continually downskilling myself. I was also cheating myself of my potential.

That hidden message from my school, I eventually realized, was not only crippling, it was wrong. The world is not an unsolved puzzle, waiting for the occasional genius to unlock its secrets. The world, or most of it, is an empty space waiting to be filled. That realization changed my life. I did not have to wait and watch for the puzzles to be solved, I could jump into the space myself. I was free to try out my ideas, invent my own scenarios, create my own futures. Life, work and organization could become a self-fulfilling prophecy, with my making the prophecies, being unreasonable.

There were risks, I knew. Inevitably I would make mistakes, maybe big mistakes. It would be sensible to take counsel, to listen to the wise, but not unquestioningly; I ought to test the temperature of the water before jumping in, but remember that every pool feels warmer once you're in it; I must learn to forgive myself for getting it wrong at times, but remember to work out why I got it wrong. A bad memory, I read to my delight, often goes with creativity. Intellectually lazy and very forgetful, I seldom have the energy to read all the experts that I should, nor the recall to quote them when I ought. It is more exciting to think that you are creating a world than to feel you are merely replicating it.

This way of thinking and living is crucial to many parts of life, if certainty no longer holds sway. It is a way of thinking which is crucial to the leadership of our businesses, our schools and our government; to relationships, to parenting and to life itself. Intriguingly, science, too, has moved away from the search for total certainty and predictability to a concern with Chaos, Creativity and Complexity. There is, it seems, space and randomness at the heart of things. If I had studied more science I might have known this earlier, but you have to work such things out for yourself if they are to have any real meaning.

Fired with excitement at how this new way of looking at the world had changed *my* life, I was, for a while, euphoric about the openings it offered to all, the possibility it held out for each one of us to invent a life, a career, an organization. Talking about it around the world, however, to organizations and their leaders, of every hue and in every sector, I came to realize that the end of certainty is not welcome news to most. Most people are not prepared for it, most would rather have chains than empty spaces, railroad tracks than prairies, even if the tracks do not lead to heaven. For many of us, the world is a confusing place once certainty is gone.

They no longer know where they want to go, or how to get there. In the world at large, affluence for some does not, after all, end up in affluence for all. The marketplace turns out to be great for trading but not for building. Families may have been a straitjacket, but at least they were a jacket, something to keep out the worst of the cold. Jobs might be boring but they filled the day. Many would like to go 'Back to Basics', as Britain's John Major sensed when he made it his rallying call this year, but it turned out that no one knew what the basics were. There is no certainty any more.

We aren't even sure what life itself is for; if, indeed, it is anything more than a genetic accident. And as for the organizations of business – is it really worth giving up the best part of your life to make the shareholders seriously rich? Why does anyone want riches anyway, once they have enough to live on? To have a headstone by my grave, inscribed 'Here lies Charles Handy, who is proud to have spent so much' is hardly my idea of immortality. There must be more to life than spending. And yet − a society, and an individual, is remembered in the end not for how they made their money, but for how they spent it. Look at the Renaissance of Italy − a flowering of all the talents that has thrilled us down the ages, made possible by the spending of guilty bankers. Life is confusing.

And so it was that I came to write the next book, *The Empty Raincoat*, which started by listing the confusions. It turned out to be a more pessimistic book than the last one, with more questions than answers. Inevitably so, because when certainty is gone we must each find our own answers, but with, I hope, the help of others. In fact, without that help, we will not only fall but in our falling will bring others down, because society and the world is now inextricably intertwined or, to put it more materialistically, producers need consumers and so had better help many others to be producers so that they can afford to be consumers. Always there is paradox. Or again, a world of empty space is an invitation to be yourself to your fullest extent, but, in the end, we need others to find meaning for ourselves.

Translating these truisms into recipes for action is not easy. It involves, I found, turning on their head some ideas with which I grew up, or, at the very least, linking them with other ideas. Compromise, for instance, not victory, is often the path to progress. Or, if compromise jars, call it balance. Organizations will need to give more freedom to individuals than they may be comfortable with if they are to retain their commitment and creativity, finding the beneficial compromise behind the corporate need for control and the individual pressure for autonomy. In my own life, there was a time when it seemed right and necessary for me to give all my time and energy to my work. 'I'm happy for you that your work is going so well,' my wife said to me one day. 'I just think that you should know that you have become the most boring man I know.' I changed the balance; less successful now, perhaps, but more interesting, I hope.

Governments would do well to heed Arthur Okun's statement that The Invisible Hand of the open market needs to be balanced by An Invisible Handshake if it is to work to the benefit of all. It is not always remembered that Adam Smith not only wrote *The Wealth of Nations*, the bible of capitalism, but also and, in his view, more importantly, *A Theory of Moral Sentiments*, in which he argued that 'sympathy', a proper regard for others, was the basis of a civilized society. Markets, for wealth and efficiency, need to be balanced by sympathy, for civilization. You won't, however, have much sympathy for those you never meet or see. We need to rub up against people different from ourselves just as much as we need to gang up with our own sort for our comfort and security. Ghettoes for the rich and ghettoes for the poor won't be for the good of all. We need to reinvent our cities, as well as our organizations, if the rich are to be persuaded to invest in the poor. If they don't, the rich may soon be poor in their turn.

These last ten years have been, for me, an intellectual journey, one that mirrored, I believe, a changing world. I moved from certainty, through an excitement with individual potential in an uncertain world, to what I now think is a necessary compromise between 'I' and 'they' to make 'we' in every sphere of life. Others may have made this journey before, but each of us has to find our own way, even if it ends in the same place. I hope that it will, because, with the unexpected end of the communist dream, capitalism is now its own worst enemy. We have to demonstrate that we can build a just society on the basis of individual freedom, a freedom which does not turn into licence, or into a tyranny of the few at the expense of the many.

I sense that we now stand at the top of the pass. Spread out below is a vast expanse, with no roads through it. We can, I suppose, each take our own individual buggies and drive off alone into the night, for good or ill. Worse, we can jump with some friends into a tank and forge together through the future, and damnation to the rest. Better it would be, I am now sure, to build roads which all can travel, but that means giving up some personal gain so that all may benefit more in the end. We won't do that, I fear, in our society, in our cities or in our organizations, unless and until we have a better idea of what the journey is all about. The Meaning of Life comes to the top of the agenda again, even if organizations want to call their bit of it a Vision Statement. In my youth I was too busy travelling to wonder much about where I was going. The older you get, however, the more concerned you are about the longer term, for we only look forward as far as we can look back. My hope, therefore, lies in the young old, those young enough to have fire still in their bellies, but old enough to care what happens to the world after that one certainty of death. People like myself, I suppose. The trouble with working things out is that you have to start to practise what you preach. Intellectual journeys don't lead to a rest house.

Tennyson said it better, when he had Odysseus call to his sailors towards the end of *his* odyssey:

Come my friends,

'Tis not too late to seek a newer world.
Push off, and sitting well in order smite
The sounding furrows; for my purpose holds
To sail beyond the sunset and the baths
Of all the western stars, until I die ...
We are not now that strength which in old days
Moved earth and heaven; that which we are, we are;
One equal temper of heroic hearts,
Made weak by time and fate, but strong in will
To strive, to seek, to find, and not to yield.

Odysseus never did sail 'beyond the sunset'. He made his way back, eventually, to Ithaca, his old home and kingdom, which he found to be in a dreadful mess. It was there, where he had come from, that he made his 'newer world'. There is no escaping. The future for us, too, is in our own place, if we can learn to see it differently, and are 'strong in will' to change it.

TWO

◆

THE COMING
WORK CULTURE

It's happening right before our eyes, a vast reconfiguration of the world of work. Entire floors of office buildings are emptying, whole layers of management are going out the window, full echelons of support staff are being told to support themselves. The *Wall Street Journal* reported last October that fully 75% of the newly jobless, a rising figure, are coming from the ranks of managers, professionals, and administrative and technical staff.

It is not because of the recession. The recession is a blip on a long-term trend in corporate organization. Driving this trend is heightened competition in the global marketplace. Price wars and quality wars are forcing companies to slim down their employment rolls to a hard core of operatives whose only function is to serve the needs of customers and to tight little nuclei of managers whose only function is to find and hold on to those customers. The result is a mighty extrusion of personnel. Employees who are not connected to the core tasks of the business – all those in-house cooks and lawyers, accountants and PR people, art directors and security guards, bank economists and ATM maintenance crews – will soon find themselves in a new relationship, if any, to their former employers. They will become more or less independent actors in the business's contractual support network – jobbers, pieceworkers, consultants, accommodators, 'temps' of all sorts and degree, all plying their different trades and skills.

From the company's point of view, this great squeeze-out makes perfect sense. Why keep people working full-time when you need them only two or three days a week, if that? Far better to let them go, then hire them back for fees, not wages or salaries. Fees are paid for work accomplished, wages and salaries for time spent – which is not always the same thing. For far too long, organizations have been full of people inventing work to keep themselves busy, occupying offices that sit there, mostly empty, for 128 hours of downtime every week. Such arrangements were feasible when markets were cosy conspiracies where prices could be set at whatever cost the buyers could bear, not, as today, at whatever figure the competition will permit management to bear. Such arrangements were also necessary when productive enterprise mostly consisted in assembling hands to assemble things. But now that businesses are more often engaged in bringing together heads to compile knowledge and information, managers no longer have to observe the unities of space, time, and task. Meanwhile, of course, factories are replacing hands with machines that work 168 hours a week and don't, usually, go on strike. Call it what you will – a liberation or an abandonment, a perestroika of the private sector or a savage new twist in the corporate struggle for existence – this great squeeze-out is causing tremendous changes in the world of work, creating new patterns of opportunity and risk, and forcing us all into new ways of thinking about jobs, careers, remuneration, and the whole shape of our lives.

At last count, the number of people in full-time jobs in organizations was less than half of all the adults of working age – and the statistic was as true of Europe as of the United States. The rest were self-employed, part-time or temporary workers, unemployed, in prison, or what the Organization for Economic Cooperation and Development so quaintly calls UDWs (Unpaid Domestic Workers) – no prizes for guessing what sex most of these were. In fact, if you reckon that 'working age' is a concept that now extends indefinitely, or at least into one's 70s, then the percentage share of those traditional full-time organizational operatives in the work force would fall even further.

What is happening here? Essentially the emerging configuration of the work world resembles something of a three-ringed circle. In the inner ring and the outer ring the occupants look quite familiar. The core is filled with corporate insiders, the sort of managers who have flourished in commercial society for centuries – entrepreneurs who give their whole lives to their business, highly trained executives who step in when the entrepreneurs wear out, and the young, totally dedicated ladder-climbers who want to replace the older executives. Also in this core group are the technicians, marketing strategists, and salespeople who serve as messengers to and from the customers, learning and satisfying their wants. This core will do very well, benefiting from the new $\frac{1}{2}$-by-2-by-3 rule of corporate fitness – half as many people on the payroll, paid twice as well, producing three times as much.

The outer ring is filled with largely interchangeable, frequently disposable workers who will most likely be no better off than they were yesterday. They are the 'somebody' in the phrase 'somebody has to do it' – our least-skilled clerks and labourers, the servants of the service sector. Many of them, perhaps an increasing percentage of the whole, will be unable to add enough value to cover their cost to the organization and will soon drop out of the work force altogether, becoming costs to society at large. Whether our society ultimately pays those costs in education, occupational training, and employment in public service or in police forces, prisons, homeless shelters, and welfare benefits is a momentous question.

It's in the middle ring that we find something new. These are the people who, by choice or circumstance, find themselves on the outside of corporate enterprise, working in. I call them the portfolio people. What I mean by this I can best explain by repeating what I told my own children when they left college. 'I hope you won't go looking for a job,' I said. I was not advocating the indolent life or a marginal one. What I meant was that rather than scurrying about looking for a corporate ladder to climb or a professional trajectory to follow, they ought to develop a product, skill, or service, assemble a portfolio that illustrates these assets, and then go out and find customers for them.

I don't propose the portfolio way of life lightly. Some of us will have little choice in the matter; others will choose it willingly – some to their satisfaction, some to their regret. Either way, entering this zone of the world of work obliges us to rethink many fundamental assumptions of our lives.

For one thing, we will have to abandon the metaphor of the *line* – always an upward-tending one, we'd like to think – as the organizing design of our autobiographies. Portfolio people can no longer think of their *line* of work, one job leading to another and better job, ending in something called success (or failure). Neither can they think of all those other lines – some called family, others called fun, still others called obligation (to society, say, or one's profession or church) – out of which, along with their line of work, people have traditionally woven the fabric of their lives.

Instead, portfolio living forces us to think in terms of the circle, something like a pie chart with different segments marked off for different occupations, each coloured for kind and degree of hoped-for remuneration. Some occupations will be paid in money, some in other kinds of reward: love, creative satisfaction, power, joy, and the like. And of course the chart will be constantly changing, the dimensions of the occupation segments expanding or contracting according to the time invested, the remuneration colours fading or brightening according to the returns on the investment, and this not only over the years of one's life but from week to week, even day to day.

Some people might call this sort of living holistic, thereby giving it a New Age resonance. But it looks to me more like the lives of the people I grew up with in rural Ireland. I never knew anyone who went off to work in an office. The people I knew were farmers working their own fields, doctors with their surgery in their front room, storekeepers living over the store, teachers living in their schools, or parsons, like my father, living in his rectory by his church. Home and office, career and hobby, workmates and playmates, all jumbled together. Perhaps history has come full circle. But whatever image sums it up best, pie chart or rural village, portfolio living most of all obliges us to think differently about the idea of a career.

For the portfolio class, career takes on a new meaning. Portfolio people put their different bits of work into folders, rather as architects do, or journalists, and sell their services through examples of their products. At times one client, one project, will fill up the portfolio. This is especially true of many people in the first stages of their careers, when they lock into an organization for experience and development. But more and more, as other responsibilities, including parenting, need time and attention, and as our powers and interests expand, our portfolios will diversify. Often, important things will never get into them. There will be no notes, for example, saying which piece of work got done easily, which was paid well, which was done for love, which was a botch (to client or creator), or which was really the work of an assistant.

This new notion of career is already catching on. The PR person, the marketing expert, even the project engineer and sales manager, are coming to see themselves somewhat as actors do, looking for good parts in new productions and not expecting or wanting any one part to run forever. Organizations, on their side, will have to offer a continuing series of good roles if they want to keep their best people. A promise of medical insurance will not be enough for the best of the portfolio careerists. They will want challenge and a chance to develop in their professional fields, as well as money, and they will move to wherever they can find these opportunities.

Self-managers of our own assets – that's what more and more of us are becoming. And in a sense this new class is being made by women, for women, and of women. This is not surprising. Women have often been less attracted to the 'inside' of organizations, if only because they long had been made singularly unwelcome there. Women have also, per-force, had to live extraordinarily flexible lives, juggling portfolios of work, family, and community. Women, too, seem to know better than men – who are usually content to empty their in-trays and go with the flow of the system – that if you want to get anything to happen in this life, you have to pick up the phone and start it happening.

What looks to me like a certainty is that we will all need our portfolios one day, men and women, insiders and outsiders. Life lasts longer now. We are as healthy at 70 as our mothers and fathers were at 50. At the same time, whatever the forecasters say, organizational employment will be ending sooner rather than later for all of us. In the organizations of the next century, as they strip down to the barest essentials, retirement will come at 55, or sooner. At that age, of course, *retirement* is ludicrously the wrong word. Most of us will have 20 more years of active life. The Troisième Age, the French like to call it, maintaining that we go through the First Age of Learning and the Second Age of Working, until we come to the Third Age of Living. But living is not all leisure; indeed, unless we are very rich, it cannot be. The Third Age will include work, preferably work of our choice, work that allows us to feel useful and valued. For almost half our working lives, then, virtually everyone will be doing portfolio work – bits and pieces, this and that, now and then – customers, not jobs.

Those who start preparing for the Third Age in their Second Age will probably enjoy it most. We should therefore – those of us who have not yet started – dip our toes into the portfolio life as soon as we can. Organizations would be wise to let their insiders do a bit of outsiding as a way of preparing them for life beyond the job. (They might encourage senior executives to begin to establish themselves as consultants in Eastern Europe, for example.) If they do not, they may find their insiders outstaying their usefulness, clinging to the false security of the only world they know in fear of the cold outside. There is no easy way to prepare for the portfolio life except to try it. And it's not so difficult. No longer do you have to do everything yourself to make your portfolio come alive. Technology puts data and skills at your fingertips, giving one woman access to accumulated knowledge that in the past could be found only in vast organizations.

Not long ago I was looking for a parking space and saw a man sitting in his car behind the wheel. 'Will you be long?' I asked.

'About three hours, I think,' he replied.

Then I saw the car phone, the portable computer, the fax, all on the seat beside him. 'Good heavens,' I said, 'you've got a whole office in there.'

'Sure,' he said, 'it's much cheaper parking here than hiring space up there.' He jerked his thumb at the high-rise office building behind us.

By the same token, I was asked some weeks ago to do a phone-in interview with a morning radio show in Baltimore, Maryland. Nothing odd about that except that where I was sitting, in the fenlands of East Anglia, it was early evening. You don't have to be in the same place to exchange information now; you don't even have to be in the same time zone.

Sociability will suffer, of course, because getting everyone together is often an expensive proposition. But sociability in the workplace is declining anyway. Last month I visited a sugar refinery where 150 people used to work shovelling the sticky stuff around in huge vats. Today the whole thing is done by machines. There is one worker on duty at a time, watching dials, with a telephone hookup to an engineer in case of emergency. The employee on duty is well paid but a touch lonely.

Then, too, we can emulate the organizations. As they no longer try to do everything themselves, we can do likewise.

Every business, big or small, is essentially now a broker, a welder together of other people's skills and products. My design-consultant daughter, for example, hires builders when she needs them. In business nowadays first comes the idea for the customer, then the brokerage to realize the idea for the customer, then the delivery of the realized idea to the customer. Ideas and brokerage do not require too much capital, just imagination, the ability to listen (to the customer), and the energy and ability to make things happen through other people.

The portfolio life will not be to everyone's taste. It maximizes freedom at the expense of security: an ancient trade-off. Without the 'drama of boss, subordination, and routine', as one economist describes organizational employment, many of us are totally lost. Some of us don't know what to do without people and papers to push around; others don't know what to do without people to push *them* around. Both are in a state of organizational dependency – 'hands', human resources to be used by others, or by the system.

The fact remains that for good and ill the portfolio life is for most of us the life of the future. Organizations are never again going to stockpile people. The employee society is on the wane. New models are needed, new role players who will make the new ways less frightening. Political society will also have to make changes: resolving once and for all that children grow up with something to sell to the world, and something also to give, one hopes. And political society must resolve, too, that the helpless and the failures in this new order do not suffer too much, or bring too much suffering.

THREE

◆

BALANCING CORPORATE POWER: A NEW FEDERALIST PAPER

One of the world's oldest political philosophies is its newest subject of interest. The European Community, the new Commonwealth of Independent States, Canada, Czechoslovakia, and many more are all re-examining what federalism really means. Businesses and other organizations are beginning to do the same. Everywhere companies are restructuring, creating integrated organizations, global networks, and 'leaner, meaner' corporate centres. In so doing, whether they recognize it or not, they are on a path to federalism as the way to govern their increasingly complex organizations.

The prospect of applying political principles to management issues makes a great deal of sense, given that organizations today are more and more seen as mini societies rather than as impersonal systems. But the concept of federalism is particularly appropriate since it offers a well-recognized way to deal with paradoxes of power and control: the need to make things big by keeping them small; to encourage autonomy but within bounds; to combine variety and shared purpose, individuality and partnership, local and global, tribal region and nation state, or nation state and regional bloc. Change a few of the terms and these political issues can be found on the agendas of senior managers in most of the world's large companies.

It is therefore no accident that Percy Barnevik, the CEO of Asea Brown Boveri, has described his sprawling 'multi-domestic' enterprise of 1,100 separate companies and 210,000 employees as a federation. Nor is it accidental that John Akers has called IBM's restructuring a move to federalism. Basel-based Ciba-Geigy recently moved from a management pyramid with a matrix designed around businesses, functions, and regions to an organization with 14 separate businesses controlling 94% of all the company's spending – a federal organization.

Although they do not always call it federalism, businesses in every country are moving in the same direction: General Electric, Johnson & Johnson, and Coca-Cola in the United States; Grand Metropolitan and British Petroleum in Great Britain; Accor in France; and Honda in Japan. Older global companies, such as Royal Dutch Shell and Unilever, went federal decades ago, pulled that way by the demand for autonomy from their overseas subsidiaries. But they, too, are always flexing their structures and fine-tuning the balance of power because federalism is not a static system.

Neither, however, is federalism just a classy word for restructuring. The thinking behind it, the belief, for instance, that autonomy releases energy; that people have the right to do things in their own way as long as it is in the common interest; that people need to be well-informed, well-inten-tioned, and well-educated to interpret that common interest;

that individuals prefer being led to being managed: these principles reach into the guts of the organization or, more correctly, into its soul – the way it goes about its business day by day. Federalism properly understood is not so much a political structure or system as it is a way of life.

It is, however, the structure that changes first, as organizations twist and turn in their attempts to cope with the paradoxes of modern business. To understand federalism at work, we first need to examine these paradoxes and the ways in which organizations are evolving to deal with them. Then a look at the five key principles of federalism will show how this particular political theory can illuminate these paradoxes and point the way to some practical action.

Every organization is different, so there will be no common or even constant solution to each dilemma. And a federal organization can be particularly exhausting to govern since it relies as much on influence, trust, and empathy as on formal power and explicit controls. But in today's complex world of interrelationships and constant change, the move to federalism is inevitable. And that which is inevitable it is best to understand so that we may profit from it.

The first paradox is that organizations need to be both big and small at the same time, be they corporations or nations. On the one hand, the economies of scale still apply. The discovery and development of new sources of oil and gas require resources that no small niche player could contemplate. Big is essential as well for pharmaceutical companies if they are to finance the massive research programmes on which their future depends. Bigness also makes an organization less dependent on a few crucial people or on outside expertise.

At the same time, businesses and nations need to be small.

Everywhere small nation states and regions are flexing their muscles and demanding more autonomy. People want to identify with something closer to them and of human scale. We want villages, even in the midst of our cities. It is no different in organizations. Small may not always be beautiful but it is more comfortable. It is also more flexible and more likely to be innovative.

This paradox, how to be big but small, dominates politics and business today. In politics, federalism has been the traditional answer, although its subtleties are not always well understood even by politicians. In business, federalism is not simple decentralization with the centre acting as a banker to the separate businesses like the conglomerates of old. That loses the advantages of scale, of being able to develop lead technologies across a range of separate businesses, of combining to purchase or bid for a major contract that might involve the skills of several businesses.

But neither is federalism a simple divisionalization, the grouping of businesses under sets of umbrellas. That leaves too much power in the hands of those holding the umbrellas and pays too little attention to local needs or to the knowledge and contacts of those out in the marketplace. Nor is it a matter of simply empowering those on the front line or in the separate countries. That ignores the expertise of people farther back or in other groupings.

Federalism responds to all these pressures, balancing power among those in the centre of the organization, those in the centres of expertise, and those in the centre of the action, the operating businesses. It is worth noting that Barnevik talks about centralized *reporting*, not centralized control, because most of his key people are not located at the centre of ABB's matrix of global business strands and national companies.

The true centres of federal organizations are dispersed throughout the operations. They meet frequently and they talk often, but they do not need to live together. Doing so would be a mistake because it would concentrate too much power in one group and in one place, whereas federalism gets its strength and energy from spreading responsibility across many decision points. ABB's situation may seem extreme, but there exists one private company, also nominally based in Switzerland, that employs 80,000 people worldwide but has no one employed in its central company.

That is not completely true. There is one person who infuses the whole organization with his personality – though not with his power – and holds everything together with his vision. The same is, by all accounts, true of Barnevik, who seems to be everywhere at once, leading seminars with his managers, prodding, questioning, inspiring, 'being a missionary', as the CEO of another global corporation once put it. Federalist centres are always small to the point of minimalist. They exist to coordinate, not to control.

Business's second paradox lies in its declared preference for free and open markets as the best guarantee of efficiency, even as its managers instinctively organize their own operations for centralized control.

Two hundred years ago, the political philosopher Edmund Burke argued that centralized power would always lead to bureaucratic procedures that ultimately stifle innovation, stamp out individual differences, and therefore inhibit growth. Yet in the interests of efficiency, businesses do their best to build identikit operations around the globe. If something works in Milwaukee it ought to work in Manchester, the logic goes, and it certainly makes it more convenient for those in the centre if it does. Also, of course, there is management's conviction that only the centre can know the whole picture, only the centre can take decisions that are in the best interest of all.

That conviction may well be true. But the costs are high, the bureaucracy disabling, the delays and demotivation crippling. That is why in many businesses the breakup value of the operations exceeds the market value of the total enterprise. The centre has a negative added value, or, to put it another way, the transaction costs of central planning and control exceed the contribution that they undoubtedly make.

'Think global, act local' may be the fashionable slogan for dealing with this paradox, but it will not work very well as long as all real power resides in what is usually still called the *Head* Office or sometimes, suggestively, the Kremlin. On the other hand, a hollow corporation can soon lack direction, standards, or any sort of cohesion.

One British furniture company had a rule that it would only grow outward, not upward. No business unit would contain more than 100 people. So as the company prospered, it built new factories and mini businesses, each autonomous, each responsible for generating its own customers and expertise, each remitting its profits to the centre and drawing on the centre – and the others – only if needed. The system worked well in the days of heady growth. But come the recession and the need to allocate scarce resources, there was no one left with the power, authority, or knowledge to make those strategic decisions. Left to themselves, the locals could not think globally, and on occasion five separate business units would be found competing against each other for the same order. Open markets, on their own, do not necessarily work any better than central planning. A bit of both is needed – the federal compromise.

'What you do not own you cannot command' sums up the next paradox: the desire to run a business as if it were yours when you cannot afford, or may not want, to make it yours. Wholly-owned business empires are becoming a thing of the past. In some countries, local representation is a matter of law, as nationalism fights back against the increasing globalization of everything. But in any case, empires are too expensive and too risky. It is cheaper and safer to expand one's scope by a series of alliances and ventures. When Pepsi-Cola and Whitbread jointly formed Pizza Hut, UK Pepsi needed Whitbread's knowledge of British leisure and property markets, while Whitbread needed Pepsi's pizza know-how. One without the other could not have done it.

Alliances, however, are notoriously difficult to manage. Part-owned companies do not take kindly to orders from a head office in another country. Neither do alliances. Rather like marriages, each one is unique, to be lived with rather than managed, better built on mutual respect and shared interests than on legal documents and tight controls. In these circumstances, power perforce has to be shared, autonomy granted, and the marriage held together by trust and common goals, two of federalism's chief ingredients.

At the same time that these paradoxes are triggering structural changes in large organizations, another force is pushing companies toward federalism. I call this force *the pull of the professionals*, and it affects the processes of an organization as much as it does the structure.

As organizations everywhere realign themselves around their core activities and competences, they are realizing that their people are truly their chief assets. Often this realization becomes apparent only in a takeover or merger, when the business, if it is any good, is typically valued at four or five times the value of its tangible assets. The difference is the potential added value of its intangible assets, the intellectual property residing in its key people.

These human assets are far from fixed. They could walk out the door next Monday. They are the new professionals, high achievers for the most part, who see themselves as having careers beyond the organization, like doctors, lawyers, and architects before them. 'My MBA is my certificate of competence and my passport,' one told me. She had still to learn that a professional's reputation is built on work completed, not on certificates obtained, but her starting motivation was clear. Such people want an organization that recognizes their individual talents and provides space for their individual contributions. They prefer small, autonomous work groups based on reciprocal trust between leader and led, groups responsible, as far as possible, for their own destiny. They would like to have it both ways, of course, preferring those autonomous groups to be part of a larger family that can provide resources, career opportunities, and the leverage that comes with size. Federalism to them is thus a way to make it big while keeping it small – and independent.

Faced with these simultaneous pressures, businesses are adapting and experimenting. In so doing, they might save themselves some pain by understanding the basic principles that have defined federalism over the centuries. For these five principles – well-established though not always well-applied – translate readily into the world of business where they can provide an organizational framework for the way the company goes about its work.

Subsidiarity is the most important of federalism's principles. It is a pity only that it is such an ugly and uncomfortable word. It means that power belongs to the lowest possible point in the organization. 'A higher order body should not take unto itself responsibilities which properly belong to a lower order body' is how a 1941 papal encyclical puts it, because subsidiarity has long been part of the doctrine of the Catholic Church. The state should not do what the family can do better is one example of the principle turned into practice. 'Stealing people's decisions is wrong' might be another way of putting it, something parents wrestle with as their children grow up.

All managers are tempted to steal their subordinates' decisions. Subsidiarity requires, instead, that they enable those subordinates, by training, advice, and support, to take those decisions better. Only if the decision would substantially damage the organization is the manager entitled to intervene. In aviation, the trainer allows the trainee pilot to get it wrong provided that the mistake will not crash the plane. It is the only way the trainee will learn to fly alone.

In the current European debate, subsidiarity means that power resides within the individual countries of the Community. Only with their agreement can Brussels exercise any authority. It is a form of reverse delegation. British Petroleum, which in effect went federal in 1990, devolving authority and responsibility to its separate businesses, had to decide which powers the centre would retain. The centre came up with a list of 22 'reserve powers' but, after discussions with the separate businesses, these were pruned down to the 10 most essential to the future direction of the company. In a federal system, the centre governs only with the consent of the governed.

Subsidiarity, therefore, is the reverse of empowerment. It is not the centre giving away or delegating power. Instead, power is assumed to lie at the lowest point in the organization and it can be taken away only by agreement. The Catholic Church works on this holistic premise when it says that every priest is a pope in his own parish. Robert Galvin does the same when he tells Motorola's sales force that they have all the authority of the chairman when they are with customers. Taken seriously, subsidiarity is an awesome responsibility because it imposes on the individual or the group what might be called 'type two accountability'.

This follows the distinction in statistics between a type one error, which, simply put, means getting it wrong, and a type two error, which is not getting it as right as it could have been. Traditionally, we have run organizations on the basis of type one accountability, making sure that no mistakes are made. Under subsidiarity, people are also judged against their type two accountability – did they seize every opportunity, did they make all the possible improvements?

To be effective, subsidiarity has to be formalized. Federal states have constitutions, negotiated contracts that set the boundaries of each group's powers and responsibilities. Organizations need contracts too. It has to be clear who can do what, how power is to be balanced, and whose authority counts where. Leave all this to chance or to personal goodwill and the powerful will steal more than they should and unbalance the whole.

Finally, subsidiarity requires intelligence and information, real-time data that is broad enough to give a total picture but detailed enough to pinpoint decision points. Before the days of electronic data interchange, true holism in business was a sham. If people are to exercise their responsibility taking account of the interests of the whole, they must have both the information that allows them to do so and enough training and knowledge to interpret the information. How else could Motorola's salespeople represent the chairman?

The centre, then, should be small and can be small because of the possibilities of information technology. Because it is small, it cannot involve itself in too much detail and will not be able to control the operating companies day to day. Subsidiarity, therefore, is self-reinforcing. In 1990, Robert Horton's first decision as chairman of British Petroleum was to move the head office out of its tower block in the city of London and to cut its numbers by more than half. The symbolism of the move was important; so was the new language for the people in the new centre (no longer the head office) – team leaders, coordinators, and advisers. British Petroleum could, and probably will, go farther and disperse some of that centre to the operating units to reinforce the next principle of federalism.

The states of a federation stick together because they need one another as much as they need the centre. In that sense a federation is different from a confederation, where the individual states yield no sovereignty to the centre and try to need nothing from their neighbours. They agree only to collaborate on certain important issues. Such things fall apart, as the new Commonwealth of Independent States in what used to be the Soviet Union may soon discover.

Interdependence is achieved partly through the reserve powers of the centre, partly by locating services or facilities needed by all in the territory of one or two. Research and development, for instance, can be located in Germany, the United States, and Japan but serve the world. The European computing centre may be run by and from France but serve all the European operating companies. In political science, this is called pluralism – many centres of power and expertise.

Federalism encourages combination when and where appropriate but not centralization. Unilever, for instance, has pulled back its European detergent manufacturing from the individual countries into one location to achieve the economies of scale possible in producing what is now a commodity. Gillette combined its European and North American marketing management in one office in Boston as a prelude to a simultaneous launch of its new Sensor razor. It is only when combination becomes excessive or is located all in one place that it offends against the principle of pluralism.

Pluralism is a key element of federalism because it distributes power, avoiding the risks of autocracy and the overcontrol of a central bureaucracy. It ensures a measure of democracy in the larger organizations because the wishes of the different players cannot be ignored. The result is the new 'dispersed centre' of federalism, a centre that is more a network than a place. There are, however, costs to this dispersion. The centre still has to be a centre, to meet and talk and share. Telephones and videoconferences are no substitutes for some real meetings. Aeroplanes and red-eyes become inevitable. The exhaustion is worth it. Paradoxically, the dispersion of the centre bonds the whole together. Units who use each other need each other.

The result is a matrix of sorts. Not the traditional matrix of functions and businesses but one in which every operating unit is accountable both to its respective global business sector and to its local region and that also draws on communal resources and services, wherever they may be located. It is a complex mix for a complex world and a mix that will be constantly changing. Federalism is and must be flexible; it can never be static.

Interdependence is unlikely, if not impossible, without agreement on the basic rules of conduct, a common way of communicating, and a common unit of measurement. If Europe ever develops into a proper federation, these will be essential requirements, just as they are in America. In corporate terms, a common law means a basic set of rules and procedures, a way of doing business. ABB has an 18-page 'bible' that is effectively its common law. Grand Metropolitan has a group of people based in the centre but travelling the world who carry with them the standards, customs, and culture of Grand Met. They are popularly known as the 'bag carriers', modern-day missionaries, promulgating the language and the law of the corporation.

A common language means not only, in most cases, American English but also a common information system so that everyone can talk – not just to one another's answering machines but also to their PCs. A common currency means simply that units of measurement must be agreed to so that oranges *can* be compared with apples around the world. Obvious though these things are, they are often forgotten in the haste to get on with the job. Too many mergers ignore them or leave them for later when they are far harder to create.

The United States and other federalist countries take this concept for granted, although it seldom percolates through to their business organizations. These, like old monarchical regimes, prefer to concentrate power wherever possible in the interests of getting things done. Federalist organizations, however, worry more that the things done by the centre may not be the right things, and they do not like to see too much power in one place or group. Now that Germany has decided to make Berlin its capital, we may see that city becoming a magnet, pulling business, finance, and the arts, as well as government, into one place. Germany would then become noticeably less federalist.

Today the management, monitoring, and governance of a business are increasingly seen as separate functions to be done by separate bodies, even if some of the membership of those bodies overlaps. This is the corporate equivalent of the separation of powers. Management is the executive function, responsible for delivering the goods. Monitoring is the judicial function, responsible for seeing that the goods are delivered according to the laws of the land, that standards are met, and ethical principles observed. Governance is the legislative function, responsible for overseeing management and monitoring and, most important, for the corporation's future, for strategy, policy, and direction.

When these three functions are combined in one body, the short-term tends to drive out the long, with month-to-month management and monitoring issues stealing the time and attention needed for governance. The big decisions then go wrong. In the Lloyd's insurance business of London, a federation made up of 179 autonomous insurance syndicates, the three functions are currently combined by law. The chairman of Lloyd's has to be a practising underwriter, that is, an executive, and Lloyd's is responsible for its own regulation. The result is a mess, a loss in 1992 of $3.7 billion for the 1989 year of account and more of the same to come. The 'names', or private individuals who have to pay these losses, are understandably clamouring for reform. Lloyd's has broken one of the cardinal principles of federalism.

Most companies are going the other way. Many have now separated the roles of chairman and chief executive and created two-tier boards, although they do not call them that, preferring to refer to the executive board as a committee or team. They also have separate audit committees and, on occasion, separate committees for monitoring the company's environmental or community responsibilities. In Britain and North America, the top board, the one responsible for governance, is not as representative of the different stakeholders as it would be in Germany or Japan. But it is increasingly seen to be the duty, particularly of the nonexecutive directors, to take those interests into account. Governance in a federal system is ultimately democratic, accountable to all the interest groups on which it depends, not just to its financiers. In the long term it cannot afford to ignore those other interests.

In a federal country, everyone is a citizen of two states, his or her own and the Union. A Texan is also an American, and the Stars and Stripes can be found waving outside the house of many an ardent Californian. A resident of Munich may be a Bavarian first and a German second, but he is both. Corporate letterheads likewise fly two flags. Some put 'a member of the X group of companies' in small letters in the corner. Others, such as Shell, give the federal logo pride of place. The layout will say a lot about the distribution of power, but both flags will always be present.

Local citizenship seldom needs much reinforcement. Indeed, the 'states' of a federal business are often themselves monarchical, led by a forceful baron. This is not inconsistent. The federal whole draws its strength from the strong leadership of the 'states' – another of federalism's paradoxes but one that ensures a strong local identity.

Increasingly, it is the federal citizenship that requires emphasis if interdependence is to be fostered. To do this, corporations add their equivalent of a national anthem to the flag, issuing 'mission statements' or 'vision and value statements' that are regularly recited throughout the federation – if not always totally believed. These are useful, symbolically, because they remind people of the larger whole and of their wider citizenship. But at their best, these national anthems provide what *The Art of Japanese Management* authors Richard Pascale and Anthony Athos call 'the spiritual fabric' of the corporation. As it happens, they are describing companies in present-day Japan. The tradition, however, is much older. In Elizabethan England, venturers went forth unfettered by authority and bound together only by their concern for 'The Queen's Great Matter'. That understanding built an empire.

Unilever has an annual occasion, popularly known as the 'O Be Joyful' day, when its senior executives from around the world assemble to hear the annual results and, more subliminally, to celebrate their second citizenship. When corporations talk of 'shared values' these days, they are recognizing that what bonds a federal system together has to be more than the need to improve the bottom line, essential though that is. It has to be some modern-day equivalent of the Queen's Great Matter. Finding that equivalent and articulating it is a major challenge for leadership.

A president also helps to bond a federation together by exemplifying the larger state and serving as its ambassador-at-large both to the outside world and, almost more important, to its own citizens. Sir John Harvey–Jones, the former chairman of ICI, understood this well. His face and laugh became familiar features in the British media and helped to give the big chemical company a human as well as a technological face. Akio Morita of Sony is another of these president ambassadors, endlessly reinforcing the core values of his federation of companies by speeches, articles, and personal visits.

Federalism is, on the face of it, a way of thinking about the structure and operations of large organizations. Leave it there and it does not make much difference to the executive or technician in Pittsburgh or Mannheim. But we cannot leave it there. The thinking about power and responsibility that animates federalism is pervasive in developed societies. The pull of professionalism ensures that this thinking reaches beyond an organization's structure into its processes, the way that individuals relate to one another and to the tasks they take on. As a result, the federal way of thinking can be extended into a set of maxims for managing in today's organizations.

Authority must be earned from those over whom it is exercised. This is the practical implication of subsidiarity. In the organizations dominated by the new professionals, you cannot tell people what to do unless they respect you, agree with you, or both. We used to teach that authority came from above, but that was when people were hired hands whose time had been bought to do the company's bidding. That day has long passed, but this so-called 'instrumental contract' still applies in many places, particularly in times of recession. Yet as more people think of themselves as professionals, with careers that span companies, purely instrumental contracts become less and less effective.

Professionals require management by consent if they are

to give their best; consent that is theirs to give or to withhold. This maxim may sound obvious, but two major and unsuspected implications follow from it. Units have to be small so that people can get to know one another well enough to earn their colleagues' respect through their records of achievement. And people have to be around long enough to build up those records. Reputation can and does precede one into a new role but then it has to be justified. We are talking, therefore of units of less than 100 people, perhaps, and of three- to five-year tenures in jobs. Organizations that think of their people as role occupants, replaceable and moveable as long as the role is properly defined, are not thinking federally. Organizations that reward success with promotion every two years are making it difficult, if not impossible, to manage with respect and by consent.

People have both the right and the duty to sign their work. Subsidiarity requires that people take responsibility for their decisions by signing their work, both literally and metaphorically. The new as well as the old professionals do just that. Your doctor is an individual, not an anonymous 'medical supervisor'. Films and television programmes end with long lists of names – the signatures of all, even the most junior, who contributed. Most journalists sign their work; so do architects, lawyers, professors, clothing designers, and artists. Consultancies' project teams now put the names of all their members on the title pages of their reports. Advertising agencies do the same. My new Swiss watch arrived with a label stating 'Gerard made this.' We may not want to know who these people are, but they want to tell us, and that is the important thing. It is a healthy trend in organizations, and it will spread as more work gets done in small, discrete groups.

A signature on one's work may be the best single recipe

for quality. For reasons of personal pride, as well as fear of recrimination, few will want to sign their names to a dud product. Federal thinking insists, however, that one's signature is a right as well as a responsibility, a demonstration that the individual has made a personal contribution. The new chief executive of an art-printing business in Britain called his work force together after one month and said, 'I am ashamed of much of the stuff that leaves this building, even if the customers seem to accept it. In future, every item will have a piece of paper headed "we are proud to have done this work" and signed by every member of the work group.' He expected an angry or at least a sullen response but instead he got cheers. 'We were ashamed too,' one worker said, 'but we thought that was all you wanted, acceptable rubbish at the lowest cost. Now all you have to do is provide the equipment so that we can do the sort of work we will be proud to sign.'

Those workers had a point. Encouraging people to sign their work does have implications. They have to have the right equipment. They have to be the right sort of people to begin with, properly trained and properly qualified. They have to know, by bench-marking or other means, what the right standards are.

Autonomy means managing empty spaces. Subsidiarity and signatures both imply a lot of individual discretion. Yet unbounded discretion can be frightening for the individual and dangerous for the organization. Groups and individuals therefore live within two concentric circles of responsibility. The inner circle contains everything they *have* to do or fail – their baseline. The larger circle marks the limits of their authority, where their writ ends. In between is their area of discretion, the space in which they have both the freedom and the responsibility to initiate action. This space exists for them to fill; it is their type two accountability.

Of necessity, individual initiatives can be judged only after the event. Organizations prefer to control and judge things before they happen. It is safer that way. It is also slower, more expensive, and it assumes that those who are higher up and farther away know better. The assumption behind federal thinking – and the empty space for individual initiative – is that those higher up may not know better. That assumption requires a lot of trust and a necessary forgiveness if the initiative turns out wrong. Where no mistakes are tolerated, no initiative will be risked. 'Forgiveness provided one learns' is a necessary part of federalist thinking. It can be a hard part to practise.

Management by trust, empathy, and forgiveness sounds good. It also sounds soft. It is, in practice, tough. Organizations based on trust have, on occasion, to be ruthless. If someone can no longer be trusted, he or she cannot be given an empty space. To keep the spirit of subsidiarity intact, those who do not merit trust must go elsewhere, quickly.

This poses a dilemma for organizations that have thought it right to guarantee jobs and careers for life to all whom they employ. If they have chosen wrongly, if trust turns out to be misplaced, they must either break the guarantee or close up the empty space professionals value so highly. It seems probable that organizations will start to require long probationary periods before they give these lifetime guarantees. Either that or they will move to more fixed-term contracts. Leaders, too, will need to be tough as well as trusting and forgiving – another federal paradox.

Twin hierarchies are necessary and useful. Twin hierarchies demonstrate the principle of interdependence at the work-group level. There is, in every organization, a clear status hierarchy. Some people are justifiably senior to others and are paid more than others because of their knowledge, experience, or proven ability. Traditionally, the most senior person in the status hierarchy leads any group on any task. That, however, makes no sense where the task requires a group of people with different skills and where one particular skill must take the lead. In an advertising agency, for instance, the young account director may be properly deferential to the wise old media buyer, but there is never any doubt about who is in the chair. In the task hierarchy, the role dictates who is who. Outside the meeting, however, the status hierarchy reasserts itself in the accustomed way.

Twin hierarchies are commonplace in professional organizations. They have to be. They are rarer in business. But they will become more common as skills become more specialized and as task groups realize that they are temporary alliances of expertise that need to make the best use of one another to get the work done – interdependence in practice. The concept has important side effects, however: by allowing the young specialist to demonstrate his or her expertise to the rest of the organization, it provides great encouragement for making that expertise as good as it can be and exposes him or her to the realities of the business. At the same time, it takes some getting used to. Not least it requires notable self-confidence from those senior in the status hierarchy if they are, on occasion, to work under the direction of their juniors.

Distinguishing between status and task hierarchies allows organizations to become much flatter without losing efficiency. The older professional organizations typically have only four levels from trainee to partner, or medical consultant, or professor, or whatever the top layer is called. The Catholic Church has bishops, priests, and deacons – and a pope who is its president ambassador. Business organizations are following suit, especially those staffed largely by knowledge workers. Four layers of status are enough, they find, as more of their work is organized in teams, each with its appropriate task hierarchy.

What is good for me should be good for the corporation. This is the twin citizenship principle brought down to the level of the individual. Professionals believe in what the Japanese call 'self-enlightenment', knowing that if they do not continually invest in their own learning and development they will be a wasting asset. What they ask of the organization is that it facilitate and encourage this process of continual learning by paying any costs and providing leaves of absence. In return, they owe a loyalty to the larger state, the organization. But as in the larger federal structures, this loyalty can no longer be taken for granted. It has to be earned and continually reinforced. If the corporation reneges on the implicit, and sometimes explicit, contract that facilitates individual development, or if it fails to recognize or take advantage of a significant piece of learning – a new qualification perhaps – the individual will feel released from any sense of obligation.

But this individualism, which provides the best guarantee of professional standards and the best engine for personal achievement, has to be harnessed to a cause that is greater than itself if it is to be truly useful. It is that larger and wider loyalty or citizenship that needs special emphasis, as it always does in federalism. St Augustine once said that the worst of sins was to be 'turned in on oneself'. It is still true today. Without that wider citizenship, the prized individualism of the new professionals can look remarkably like selfishness.

Federalism reverses a lot of traditional management thinking. In particular, it assumes that most of the energy is out there, away from the centre, and down there, away from the top. Power, in federalist thinking, is redistributed because no one person and no one group can be all-wise, all-knowing, all-competent. Monarchy is risky, acceptable only in times of crisis, as once at Chrysler. Bureaucracy is stifling. Better to let 1,000 flowers bloom, even if some of them turn out to be weeds. Paradoxically, although federalism wants no all-powerful monarch at its centre, it needs strong leaders in its parts. Choosing those leaders and developing them will always be one of the centre's closely-guarded reserve powers. You cannot, however, make a federation strong and keep it growing just by keeping it small. The independent bits, be they individuals, clusters, business units, or separate companies have to feel and be part of a greater whole.

Federalism is not simple. It matches complexity with complexity. It is always tempting to seek to impose a unitary authority and a unitary system on a set of complex purposes; but to do so ignores the necessary variety of the bigger world in which all corporations today are players. It would be akin to turning harmony into unison. Federalism is in tune with the times – times that want to value and respect diversity and difference, times in which people want to do their own thing and yet be part of something bigger, times in which they look for structure but not imposed authority.

Tried and tested, often to the point of failure, in the political world, federalism has great added value as an organizational concept. The wheel does not have to be reinvented for our corporations. We know how federalism is supposed to work. Making it happen, however, is something else again. History is not overfull of examples of monarchies or oligarchies voluntarily turning themselves into federations. Federations typically arise when smaller states need to combine and yet retain their identity. Only after war or revolution do oligarchies turn federal. Here, therefore, there are no good models. We must proceed as best we may.

To do so requires determination at the top, the will to give some power away in order to gain momentum. That will be easier if all concerned know what is happening and why, if they understand the thinking that lies behind the changes. Understanding is always a good lubricant for change. With that determination and that understanding our corporations may yet add a chapter to the textbooks of political science by providing examples of voluntary federalism.

FOUR

◆

WHAT IS A COMPANY FOR?

MICHAEL SHANKS MEMORIAL LECTURE, 1990

I was due to meet with Michael Shanks a week after his untimely and unexpected death in 1984. I do not now remember what the meeting was to be about; it could have concerned any number of things because Michael was the ultimate portfolio person. At ease in boardrooms, government offices or consumers' campaigns, he bestrode the different citadels of our business society, concerned always and only to make it a better society. His passing left a big gap in the lives of many.

I was delighted and honoured to be asked to deliver this first Michael Shanks Memorial Lecture and the topic I thought appropriate in his memory was clear: in this changing world we have to face up to the question 'What is a company really for today?' Do our rules and laws and institutions reflect that purpose or do they, perhaps, get in its way?

I am going to argue that some of the rules of our business game do today get in the way of its well-intentioned players. I shall even suggest that those rules and traditions are causing us to score some own-goals and to shoot ourselves in our collective feet (if I may mix my metaphors). I shall in the process trample on one or two precious myths, hallowed though they are in our corporate mind-set. I really do believe that we may have got it wrong and that we should at least question received wisdom. It is, of course, easier to raise the questions than to give the answers. I will dare only to point to the directions in which I think the answers may lie, because they won't be simple answers or easy ones, but to my mind it would be a great step forward to argue that some new answers were needed at all. Things do outlive their purpose, and what was once sensible may now seem crazy. We do not have to be slaves to our history.

When I started to consider this topic I realized that I was treading in illustrious footsteps. It is nearly 18 years since the Watkinson Committee reported its deliberations on the responsibilities of the British Public Company. It said many sane and sensible things, but fine words do not, in this instance, seem to have buttered any parsnips. I am delighted to see George Goyder here tonight because it was his book *The Just Enterprise* (published in 1987) which set me thinking about all this, intertwining as it did in a marvellous way the just enterprise and William Blake. Earlier this year another book, this time by Sir Adrian Cadbury, on the company chairman, also examined some of the issues as they look to one well-intentioned player, the former chairman of a big and concerned company. Recently, too, there has been a spate of seminars, talks and articles on short-termism in and around the City. I see short-termism as a symptom of a much bigger problem but the arguments have been interesting. To me most helpful were the survey on capitalism by the *Economist* in May 1990 and a recent publication from the Institute of Public Policy Research on takeovers and short-termism. I have also found most helpful my talks with Philip Baxendale who has spent much of the last ten years trying to bend the rules of the game as they currently exist to make possible his vision of a just enterprise in the Baxi Partnership. I have named the most illustrious and helpful of the footsteps to follow but there are many more. They demonstrate that there is a growing sense of unease in many quarters about the unintended consequences of being in business.

The topic, however, was given a new urgency for me by a recent visit to South Africa and meetings with the African National Congress, and then a trip to Hungary. In the first country they look with some suspicion on the institutions of capitalism but recognize that a healthy democracy needs a healthy business sector, while in Hungary they yearn for the institutions of a free market but are dismayed to find that the first results are 40% inflation, pollution and growing unemployment. In both countries they were asking what was a company really for – itself or society? The answer is, I hope, both. But is the pursuit of self-interest bound to be for the common good or do we need to recognize that Adam Smith lived in a simpler world, at a time when, for instance, you loved both yourself and your neighbours because you knew them and could not ignore them? Do we need new rules for a new and more complicated world?

What is a company for? In my American business school in the sixties the answer was clear, it was inscribed above the blackboard in every class, it was 'to maximize the medium-term earnings per share'. Not short-term earnings, mark you, and not optimize, but maximize. From this all else flowed, given, of course, a perfect market and an intelligent one and managers who were clever, energetic and wise – something to which my business school was attending. Looking back, it is amazing that we never challenged either the statement or its premise.

Yet my own life before that should have given it the lie. I had been a lowly regional manager in a distant outpost of a great oil company. I suppose I saw the published results of the company but its earnings per share, its profitability, did not keep me awake at night, nor get me leaping out of bed in the morning. I knew, of course, that any project proposals must earn a rate of return above a stated cost of capital, and every proposal of mine always did of course, but I was never around long enough to see if the reality lived up to the proposal. I had other things on my mind and I don't just mean my social life.

I had, for instance, to deal with the village of Kapit and its headman, 200 miles up the Rejang River in Borneo. There had been an unusually large crop of the wild nuts that are used in the making of chocolate and the tribes-people had loaded them into their canoes and sped down-river with their outboard motors to sell them to the merchants in Kapit. Now they wanted to get back but I had failed to anticipate their demand and the town was out of petrol. It would take a week for the steamer to come up-river with the new supplies. We were the only oil company there. The little town had no space and no food for all those people. I was not the most popular or respected white man around. I'm afraid that the possibility of milking my monopoly position and trebling the price of the petrol when it did arrive did not occur to me. In fact, I sold it at a 50% discount to say I was sorry. In Kapit, that week, my concern for my customers far outweighed my consideration of earnings per share.

Not so, my business school would have argued. They come to the same thing. If you had exploited your customers, you would in the end have lost your monopoly because a competitor would have come in. In their perfect world, perhaps, but not in Kapit in the sixties. The cost of entering that market was prohibitive relative to any likely profits. No – I had a little local monopoly, the dream of any small business, but, if I'm honest, it was my own self-respect which drove me, and the need to preserve my reputation as the company's representative. The connection with maximum earnings per share was very remote, very long-term, very intellectual, very unreal.

With this everyday story of business folk I am making the rather obvious point that out there in the real world of business it is producing things for people on time, in good condition, and at a fair price which matters, without mucking up a decent town like Kapit, or upsetting the local government, or taking unreasonable advantage of a short-term profit opportunity. I was not there, I felt, to maximize the earnings of some anonymous shareholders. I had, I was sure, a much more serious social function, as I told a maiden great-aunt back in Ireland who complained that I was the first member of her family to go into trade. It was a form of social contract but it needed profits to make it work and go on working. That, too, I knew.

My business school in America was wrong, I am now convinced. The principal purpose of a company is not to make a profit – full stop. It is to make a profit in order to continue to do things or make things, and to do so even better and more abundantly. Late in those same sixties Jim Slater came to talk to the students at the new London Business School. He was at the height of his fortunes and he was happy to explain his secret to the young men and women. 'I am the only person in British business,' was his message, 'who is interested in making money. All the rest make money in order to do something else. That makes it easy for me to look at assets and investment decisions in a totally uncluttered way.'

Three years later his business was finished. I never got to ask him if he still felt that way.

To say that profit is a means to other ends and is not an end in itself is not a semantic quibble, it is a serious moral point. In everyday life, those who make the means into ends in themselves are usually called neurotic or obsessive, like that great-aunt of mine who was meticulous about how we were dressed and adorned for church each Sunday, the way we knelt and the prayer book we carried, but seemed not to understand or be interested in the theology of it all, the content of the preaching or the praying. In ethics, to mistake the means for the ends is to be turned in on oneself, one of the greatest of sins, said St Augustine.

Let us be clear, profits – and good profits – are always essential, and not just in business. But the myth dies hard, the myth that profit is the purpose. I attended a gathering of senior managers in one corporation where they were discussing their new mission statement, with its declaration of intent to serve customers, society, employees and the environment with as much enthusiasm as its shareholders. The chief executive, pressed to make a personal statement of priorities said: 'When it comes to the crunch I'm a bottom line guy.' The room cheered. He was macho. Why, I wondered, did they cheer? They weren't shareholders, the company was not in financial peril, there was nothing in it for them. Wouldn't it have been more exciting to be the best in their industry, or the most innovative, or the most respected, or even the biggest? But no, they wanted to be the most profitable. 'Profits is the principal yardstick,' said the Watkinson Committee, but yardstick of what for what, and how can a yardstick be a purpose? It is like saying that you play cricket to get a good batting average. It's the wrong way round. You need a good average to keep on playing cricket in the first team.

The second myth is equally pervasive, that those who pay the money own the company. In this case the purpose of the company would be to meet the requirement of the owners, which might or might not be to maximize the medium-term earnings per share. I have, for instance, been impressed by the sense of trusteeship that you sometimes find in long-standing family businesses. 'We had to sit out two world wars,' said the head of one such business in Belgium, 'but they counted on us,' and he pointed down to the roofs of the little town that surrounded his plant which had been, for generations, the principal employer in that place. Most shareholders in a public company, however, do not survey their corporate holding from the top of the factory. They are more akin to punters at the races, as the *Economist* once described them, placing their money on their financial runners.

To expect the punters who had backed the bay gelding to stay with that horse throughout its career, or to give their advice to its trainer, would not be reasonable. If they don't like its form, they transfer their money to another. Punters or speculators they may be, owners in any real sense they cannot be. Nor, in my view, will devices to lock them into their bets by tax incentives or legal requirements be more than an irritation in a free market. Andy Cash and his co-authors call this 'throwing sand' into the market and that, I think, is about all that it would do. Nevertheless, those punters have an extraordinary privilege. They are, for the price of their bets, given a vote from time to time in the auction ring as to who should own their horse. This means that they need to be wooed, continuously, for who knows when the bell for the auction ring may toll? Every company, under these rules, is effectively up for sale every day.

It is argued that the constant possibility of the auction ring concentrates the mind of the trainer. It certainly diverts his attention to the price and away from the animal – the company in this case. I asked one supermarket chairman why he was expanding so energetically into France and Belgium, buying up competitors wherever possible. Was it to prepare for the enlarged market of 1993? No, he replied, we want to make ourselves so big and so complicated that no one will be tempted to swallow us up. The best defence against being bought is, it appears, to buy. Yet all the evidence suggests that the bidder does worse, most times, than the loser at the end of the day. It is, as someone said, a funny old world.

It is worse than that, it is a form of suicide. During the ten years 1972–82 one-third of the biggest 730 quoted companies in Britain changed ownership, with all the complications and expense and distractions which such a change involves. The comparable figure for Japan was under 8%. In Germany, of the 450 companies quoted on their stock exchange only 30 or so are actively traded. The auction ring is seldom used. In contrast, remember that there are 2,400 companies listed on the London Stock Exchange, almost all of them candidates for the auction ring at any time.

To keep the punters happy we have to pay them. UK dividends are nearly twice as high as German dividends and three times as high as Japanese. That raises the effective cost of capital since most large companies would like to finance their investment out of retained earnings. If you don't have enough of these you have to borrow and even if you do have enough the profitability of the investment has to beat the cost of the dividend to make it worthwhile. So it is that British companies currently look for a return of 24% on new projects, American companies 24%, German companies 15% or so and Japanese ones 8%. Guess which countries invest most in long-term manufacturing plant and which go for the less capital-intensive service industries. It is not due to stupid or shortsighted management. It is the pressure of the auction ring.

Some say that making the managers and perhaps also the workers into the owners removes the pressure of the auction ring. But the history of management buy-outs in recent years suggests that owner-managers are just as susceptible to large offers as anyone else. I have known quite a few who profess a dedication to long-term stewardship in October, only to be out to pasture, richer by several millions, in November. Others look to create a consortium of proper owners, banks, other companies, institutions who will effectively guarantee the long-term existence of the company, leaving the punters to flutter, in the margin. Pension funds, however, who own over half of British shares, are directly responsible for other people's monies and have always shied away from so locking themselves in. In America, in fact, they are actually prohibited from sitting on the boards of companies. Acting in unison they might be persuaded to change their ways, but it would be a fundamental change. And as for individual shareholders, one forecast predicts that the last individual shareholding in Wall Street will be sold in 2,003. The idea that we are becoming a nation of small shareowners is, I'm afraid, a myth.

More fundamentally, perhaps we should ask the basic question. Why should those who pay the piper call the tune to such an extent? It does not have to be that way. The financier could be treated as we treat the providers of a mortage on our house. They hold the deeds. If we default they can sell it over our heads but only if we default on our agreed payments. Those agreed payments are equivalent to a fixed dividend. The financiers' basic security is partly the estimated income stream or profits of the occupier, partly the underlying value of the building, which it is hoped increases over time. Of course, the mortgage company is locked into the deal for twenty-five years or so. The shareholder could and should be able to take his money out at will.

It works that way, or seems so to me, in Japan, where shareholders are effectively preference debenture holders, paid a dividend related to the par value of the share. The dividend is effectively fixed and is low but is seldom if ever passed. A Japanese company will borrow to pay the dividend, something that is anathema to our practices.

More fundamentally still, I want to ask how and why the concept of property ever entered the debate. George Goyder argues persuasively that in English law the corporation is something different from its shareholders and quotes Lord Justice Evershed summing up a case in 1947: 'Shareholders are not in the eyes of the law part owners of the undertaking. The undertaking is something different from the totality of its shareholdings.' He also points to the government's wartime takeover of Short Brothers when the courts also held that the shareholders did not own the company and were not therefore necessarily entitled to the full asset value of the company. My legal friends are not sure that this is the last word on this matter and believe that the law has not fully made up its mind, or, to put it another way, might overrule its precedents.

My reasoning is much simpler. Companies used to be physical assets, run by families and their helpers. Nowadays they are largely people, helped by physical assets. Owning people is, I think, wrong. Buying and selling people is wrong. The concept is out of date, just as the idea that a man owned his wife is now out of date. In Victorian times the concept of limited liability was a wonderful piece of social invention, which enabled the family company to strut the globe. No one there thought of the resulting paradox, that owners by law have limited liability. How odd, when you stand back and look at it. The more I reflect on it, the more I think that we are today the victims of our ancestors' creativeness, that the idea of a company as a piece of property is fairly bizarre, and that the idea that those who bet on it can sell it is just crazy and may be costing our children their livelihoods. I would like it to be another myth that bites the dust.

Where does this get us? To a version of stakeholder theory no doubt, in which all those with some interest in the company have some say in its conduct and future? I do not, myself, like the idea. I don't really know who all the stakeholders are or who would properly represent them. Financiers of various types I can see, and employees. Customers clearly have a stake but how would their interest be represented other than through the marketplace where, in an open market, if such a thing really exists, they can vote with their feet? And the surrounding community, the environment, society at large? Stakeholders' language is a nice way of talking about the balancing act that companies have to perform, but I don't think, myself, that it answers the question 'what is a company for?' except in a very blurred way. It is certainly difficult to see how one could give it any teeth.

Except there are some new straws in the wind. The 1985 Companies Act requires directors to have a proper concern for their employees. That's just 'rhubarb, rhubarb' might be one slightly cynical reaction. But enter the accountants who have until now put people down as costs in the profit and loss statement, costs being things you try to minimize, with as much proper concern, of course, as you can muster. People, however, are now becoming more than mere 'hands' or 'temporary role occupants'. They increasingly represent valuable 'intellectual property'. Slowly the auction ring for companies is realizing that assets don't have to be made of bricks or steel or wood but can be made of brain. The misbegotten concept, property, has once again been trusted, but this time in effect to put people on the balance sheet as assets, not on the profit and loss as costs. It happens in the auction ring where companies are valued way beyond the worth of their physical assets and you cannot account for the difference with 'goodwill' or 'Research and Development in the pipeline' or 'patents pending' or 'brands', all of which are also part of intellectual property. People matter more now. Companies are uncomfortably aware that people are assets which could walk out of the door. Now *there* is a reason for showing proper concern for our employees.

Or take the environment. Accountants are beginning to realize that there are some gaps in their view of the world. For instance, in accounting, ownership does not have the notion of stewardship attached to it. In fact, under accounting principles, if you own something you are entitled to destroy it. Furthermore, if no one owns something then that something has no price, like air, sea or those things not reflected in the price of land, such as its ability to support life. Companies have been getting away with murder because thinking about the environment has not been in our scheme of things. Long ago it did not matter too much perhaps because there was an awful lot of land, sea, air and forests. Taking a bit of them for free was, maybe, one of those victimless crimes. No more. But the trouble is, that what is not counted does not count where it hurts, in the accounts. We may therefore expect a lot of pressure from the environmental lobbies for the accountants to fill in the gaps in their system. It has already been felt with the Pearce Report prepared for Chris Patten when Secretary of State for the Environment. Accountants have, unintentionally, skewed our idea of the world. Now they have a chance to set it straight again. I hope they will.

Even with these new numbers, however, I do not see that the stakeholder concept provides a sensible answer to the question 'what is a company for?' It may be analytically convenient to say that the company is working for all the stakeholders, but that does not tell you what to do or where to go, if you are the chairman. Inevitably, one or other of the stakeholders has priority and, given our current system, it is going to be the shareholder. Stakeholders become, then, the constraints upon the maximization of profits. That too easily becomes 'do what you have to do to satisfy the other stakeholders, then go for profit'. Back in Borneo I would still have been dissatisfied. Profit I would still see as the necessary but not sufficient condition for my company's continued existence and I would still be looking for its driving purpose.

I see the company as operating in a bounded space, a sort of hexagonal ring, surrounded by competing pressures from financiers, the employees, the customers, the suppliers, the environment and the community – the so-called stakeholders. There is no easy way to square the circle, or the hexagon. Undirected, the company will bounce from one side of the ring to the other, and many do – the oldest law of organizations is the pendulum. This time it swings six ways. Within that ring of forces I want to see the development of the 'existential corporation'. By that I mean the corporation whose principal purpose is to fulfil itself, to grow and to develop to the best that it can be, given always that every other corporation is free to do the same. It owes something to each of the ring-holders, but is owned by no one. It is in charge of its own destiny, and it is immortal or would like to be. It is not a piece of property, inhabited by humans, it is a community, which itself has property. It also has shares, traded publicly, bought by punters, but those punters have limited powers. They cannot go into the auction room unless the company defaults.

Communities have members not employees. Or rather, if they do have employees they are people outside the community not inside. Communities like all human kind need to grow and develop or they die. (Properties can and do remain static.) But they don't have to grow in size. Last month, in northern California, I had a blissful day as a wine tourist. I spoke to the owner manager of one winery. He was passionate about the future of his winery, but he wanted it to be better not bigger, and he needed lots of profits to make that possible. Businesses seem always to want to grow bigger, perhaps because their managers want bigger empires, perhaps because that makes them less easy to be bought. They miss a trick or two I sometimes feel, for bigger is not always better, or more profitable. But communities cannot be bought, except with the consent of their members, and doing the same only better is what has motivated craftsmen, artists and professionals down the ages, so it cannot be easily disparaged.

A community responsible for its own destiny, not to be bought except with its consent, is on the face of it a licence for management to do as it pleases. After the constraints of its bounded space have been met, it is accountable only to its members. This kind of self-determination has been a charter for scoundrels through the ages, or so it will be argued. I would agree that some form of authority is necessary through whom the management would be accountable – a board of trustees, perhaps, whose task is oversight not direction, with the ultimate power to replace the management should they fail in their task of growing the community. If this seems close to the supervisory boards of Germany, I would be tempted to say, 'Well, why not, it doesn't seem to have done them too much harm?' but there are other variants, including Tricker's notion of a twin board, half non-executive, which meets separately for some of the time with clearly defined duties, and half executive. An independent chairman presides over them both when they meet as one. The details, however, are less important than the principle, that the board of trustees holds the accountability of the membership of the corporate community within that hexagonal ring.

It is my belief that the businesses of Germany and Japan are thought of more as communities than as properties. They see themselves as immortal and plan for 'life beyond the grave', as one of them so nicely put it. That in turn gives a sense of security to its members who in turn are likely to think beyond the grave, without worrying about that one in three chance that the business will be sold over their heads in the next ten years. They will be prepared to sit out two world wars, for the survival of the community is to them of first importance, and they will make sure to honour their commitments to their financiers, even if they have to borrow to do it, because only if they default can the financiers move in. They will invest in their own development and they will grow the children in the local school because there will still be life beyond the grave. They will take care of their environment because it may be their own grandchildren's environment, and they will invest heavily in research, development and innovation because in that lies the hope for their children. That's what they do in Germany and Japan, for the most part, and I don't think that it is just a Germanic characteristic or a Japanese one, I think it is due to the way they think of a company, and practise it. Julian Franks, a colleague of mine at the London Business School, described on the BBC *Analysis* programme last week how, when German companies took over other German companies, nearly always by agreement, they did not close plants and cut staff but instead invested more in training, research, new equipment. New management had come in to grow the community, not to make the most of the property. It really is a different way of thinking.

But if the company as a self-governing community, not a piece of property, is such a good idea, why don't we see more of them? The answer is striking. George Goyder gives it in the first chapter of his book. Philip Baxendale reminded me of it the other day. It is given in quotation from Lord Eustace Percy in 1944:

> Here is the most urgent challenge to political invention ever offered to the jurist and the statesman. The human association which in fact produces and distributes wealth, the association of workmen, managers, technicians and directors, is not an association recognized by the law. The association which the law does recognize – the association of shareholders, creditors and directors – is incapable of production or distribution and is not expected by the law to perform these functions. We have to give law to the real association and to withdraw meaningless privilege from the imaginary one.

Having read that out I am conscious that all my preamble was unnecessary. The point is that the rules do not allow for a wealth-creating community.

What then can we do? We can work within our existing rules and exhort our managers to work as if they were an immortal community responsible for its own destiny, paying proper heed to the hexagonal space and the six stakeholders. Many large companies are trying to do this. They produce statements of vision and values, establish social responsibility departments, care for the environment and plan to be in business for the indefinite future. My feeling is, however, that they are forever looking over their shoulders. We are asking them to play fair when the rules of the game allow everyone else to play rough. It is unfair. No wonder that they sometimes pay only lip service to the other stakeholders and pander to the short-term needs of the punters, just in case. In the world of mega-millions, after all, almost no one is immune.

Alternatively, we can seek to build truly self-determining communities under our existing property rules. The John Lewis Partnership is one very well-known example. The Baxi Partnership is another. The trustees of that partnership own a minimum of 51% of the shares on behalf of the workers. They will sell only if disaster threatens but immortality is their aim. The workers can directly own another third of the shares, to hold or to sell. The Partnership Council has twelve elected members who represent the interests of the current partners (note the word) and four trustees who represent the interests of the future partners. Their job together is to oversee in general terms the board of directors who run the business.

These two organizations, and a few others like them, genuinely seek to control their own destinies, to look beyond the grave and beyond the boundaries of their sites. But their shares are not publicly traded, they are not exposed to the auction ring and they cannot therefore be example to all of us. Likewise I know family businesses which run benevolent dictatorships for the benefit of whole communities. They, too, look beyond the grave and some of them have taken their shares to the stock exchanges. They, however, are exposed to the chances of heredity. Not all heirs or heiresses are destined to be great business leaders and too often they fall foul of what my Italian friends call the third generation malaise, when the talent peters out.

I am persuaded, now, that small experiments and examples at the edge will never be enough, that we need a wholesale review of the governance of our companies, that asking managers to do it despite the rules is unfair, and that playing to the rules will inevitably emphasize the short-term, increase the costs of our investments and put us at a disadvantage to our competitors. What precise form that governance should take I do not know, but I suspect that at this point the principles are more crucial than the details.

That is my short-term worry. My long-term worry is that property prevails over community. As the world shrinks and companies aim for global reach, property will inexorably annex communities. Paradoxically, the Anglo–American system which, I have argued, works less well for everyone than the German or Japanese models, may prevail, driving the whole world into a fever of short-term speculation, forcing companies to become asset traders rather than wealth producers, and leaving Adam Smith's invisible hand to do a lot of probably unavailing overtime.

You will notice that I still have not answered my question 'what is a company for?' I will now respond that I cannot answer it. It is something that each corporate community

CHARLES HANDY

must do for itself, but we must set them free, legally, to do so. To talk of profits is no answer because I would say 'of course, but profits for what further purpose?' Talk of meeting the requirement of the stakeholders I would also regard as a necessary but not sufficient condition of existence. To have survived is not, in my view, sufficient justification for a life, either for oneself, or for one's corporate community. To make that life worthwhile one must, I feel, have a purpose beyond oneself.

What that purpose is has to be the major concern for my boards of trustees, and they should think laterally. If all aim to be number one, then 99% will be disappointed. You don't need to be big to be great, or even big to be global these days. I think I would say to these trustees, as I would to any individual that what you are is as important as what you do, and will last longer in the hearts and minds of people. A company is not an instrument, it is, or should be, a living and growing community. There is a difference.

I have said some moderately heretical things this evening. They are:

1. Profits are a necessary but not sufficient condition of success. The bottom line should be a starting post not a finishing post.
2. Owners with limited liability will never be owners, only punters, so don't expect too much from them. Turn them into mortgage men instead.
3. Stakeholder interests will not count unless they can be counted, seriously. Accountants to the rescue please.
4. Owning people is wrong. Companies are collections of people these days; they are communities not properties.
5. The law does not recognize this. It should.

6. Asking our managers to behave better than the rule book is unfair and unrealistic, so let us change the rule book.
7. If we don't, we shall endanger our children's future, and maybe even bring down our opponents with us.

Above all I want to say that in a time of change we must always question whether the things that used to work will work so well in future. We must not be slaves to our history but trustees of our destinies. Our businesses are too precious to be lost because we have not dared to question the past, or to dream the future. Let us start now, before it is too late.

DISCUSSION

DONALD B. BUTCHER (Management & Engineering Consultant): You have equated shareholders throughout your talk with punters. I believe this to be misleading. At least one should distinguish between private and institutional shareholders. My personal experience of private shareholders in big companies and in small, unquoted companies – particularly family businesses – is that they are loyal and keenly identified with the success of the company. The problem is that too few companies make significant efforts to engage and maintain private shareholder support.

THE LECTURER: I am a great advocate of family business. The strength of Germany lies in medium-sized family businesses that are not included on the stock exchange. Shareholders in that sense do want an immortal company. In the larger public companies, even if the shareholders are interested as individuals, I find it difficult to conceive that they can have any influence and I was very discouraged by the American forecast that there won't be any shareholders in ten to twelve years' time.

DR DAVID BUDWORTH (Self-employed): In his lecture Professor Handy made one or two slightly uncomplimentary remarks about accountants. I am not an accountant but I find that at the moment most of the intelligent thinking about business is coming from the accountants and accountancy bodies.

THE LECTURER: I was only uncomplimentary about accountants in the past and I agree that accountants are now realizing that they have a lot to contribute. I applaud all the initiatives currently coming from the accountancy bodies.

SIR GEOFFREY CHANDLER (Industry Adviser, RSA): What are the stimuli to bring about change in the short and medium term? Stimuli within the company include the exercise of leadership. A potential external stimulus is the market: the market operates on information and at the moment the information provided is basically financial, not concerned with training and qualifications. If there were a compulsory human audit, and indeed an environmental audit, then you would begin to get the market working on information addressed to the medium and longer term. Other external stimuli are regulation and law. The Watkinson Report has sat on the shelf for nearly 20 years, but is still relevant in many respects.

THE LECTURER: I think that the most hope lies in the internal side of the companies. If more chairmen, managing directors and chief executives saw their company as an immortal community and, therefore, accepted the need to invest in its surrounding stakeholders and its future, things would begin to change. Too many of our companies are, in a sense, asset traders and proud of it. A slight change of language might do a lot to create a different atmosphere. In the end, however, I am cynical enough to think that if we don't change some of the rules nothing much will change. The fine words of the Watkinson Report will just go on being fine words. I would like business to begin to say to rule makers, 'You are putting us at a competitive disadvantage and we actually need desperately to change those rules.'

ANNE FERGUSON (Management Editor, *The Independent on Sunday*): I would like to question the assumption that immortality is possible for companies, or desirable. There are natural life-cycles for everything from the individual to governments and civilizations. The company is a relatively new organization. What do you suggest is a natural life-cycle for a company?

THE LECTURER: Not many companies that I know deserve immortality at the moment but I would rather they died than were gobbled up by other people before they were even sick. I want companies to aim for immortality, though few will probably achieve it. I don't know what the natural life-cycle is. It seems at the moment to be something like 40 or 50 years for big companies which isn't even close to immortality but is something to aspire to. You must plan beyond the grave because if you don't, you won't invest in long-term developments. When companies take on people it is implicitly for 45 years and yet most don't last that long. If you have really taken people on for 45 years, you ought to make a huge investment in them.

PETER MORGAN (Director General, Institute of Directors): I did not wholly agree with your thesis because you had not given enough evidence about the failures you described. By contrast, Paul Marsh's recent publication on short-termism showed quite a healthy situation. Nonetheless, the Institute of Directors has just commissioned a study into company law to see whether the laws devised to help float railway companies in the nineteenth century are necessarily what companies will need in the twenty-first century.

You referred to the strength of the private company sector on the continent. The British family company has been destroyed since the war by inheritance tax and corporation tax. To rebuild that essential business base we need tax reforms.

You talked about the short-termism of shareholders but the main shareholders are the institutions and institutional shareholdings are held on average for about four years. I know this as a director of an insurance company. This is not quick in and out punting.

In my experience I have found that the ethos of the company is the focus on survival. When you have got over the problem of survival there may also be an opportunity to thrive but the truth is that most factors in the company environment tend to cause it to fail. Successfully running a company is not like administering a bureaucracy. Companies must win every day in the marketplace and conditions change every day in the market. The stakeholder plays a role in terms of the pressure he brings to bear on the bottom line which is the ultimate measure of company survival but the stakeholders are absolutely essential partners. Any company that is not working in a partnership to survive through the co-operation of suppliers, distributors, employees, customers and the surrounding community would, in fact, fail.

THE LECTURER: I don't disagree except to say that I wish companies would plan beyond survival. The companies I see that are focusing only on survival do not in some cases deserve to have a mandate.

PETER MORGAN: I don't mean just surviving the recession until the second half of 1991 but anticipating technologies and markets, consumer preferences, social factors which affect employment, maintaining a vibrant formula of success, and looking as far forward as appropriate.

THE LECTURER: Maybe that is what I call assuming immortality.

GEORGE GOYDER CBE: Thank you for the kind things you said about my book. Your final quotation was part of the 1944 Riddell Lecture given by Lord Eustace Percy and I agree that it is still as valid as when he wrote the words. From your review I was moved to think of the doctrine of trust. I believe we need a legal instrument which is based on trust, and trust is trusteeship. I see the future of large companies involving a supervisory board, which is responsible to the trustee function, while the ordinary board gets on with the management. England is the country which developed the idea of trust beyond all others. Reading F. W. Maitland in his work at Cambridge on trusts made me realize that this was a principle which was part of our British inheritance. We ought to return

to it in finding a way of balancing the hexagonal responsibilities.

THE LECTURER: The idea of trusteeship is very important in
my scheme of things.

G. R. ELLERTON (Personal Banking Director, Midland Bank
plc): Why do you think so little progress has been made to
realizing your very seductive vision? Is there some social,
cultural, or political factor at work which allows more to
develop in Germany and Japan as opposed to in Great
Britain?

THE LECTURER: It is the problem of having an undisturbed
past. We just accept that this is the way of doing things. We
don't stand back and ask 'Is it any longer sensible?' It is very
good for societies to be disrupted from time to time and it is
interesting that people who lose wars sometimes in the end
come out of them quite well.

JOHN FARAGO (Fellow of the Society): Have you any comments
on the apparent failure of the co-operative movements?

THE LECTURER: The co-operative movements don't quite fit
what I am talking about. They come out of the slightly
different ethos which is about a style of management rather
than the ownership of companies and treating the company as
a community. The co-operative movement is about the way
you run that community. They are idealistic and perhaps
slightly naïve about how you run communities. So I think it is
a fault in the management practices not the ownership status.

Stuart ROCK (Editor, *Director* magazine): Would you say that graduates emerging from, say, the London Business School would be cheering this lecture to the rafters? How do you see the task of educating the education system to play a part in effecting change?

THE LECTURER: The students I meet in London fall into two categories: about 70% of the class are very content to work within the existing system because they can see how they can thrive in it. Another 30% genuinely feel it is an odd way to run a country but they also wonder whether change will come in their lifetime and they tend to put it on one side which is a pity. There is a quiet secret minority, maybe a majority, out there who I want to stand up and say 'This is a bit odd.'

A MEMBER OF THE AUDIENCE: Following the Brinton Report and fears from the government and public about global warming and other major aspects of environmental deterioration, all parties in this country and the international community are committed to achieving sustainable development nationally and globally. How do you fit your new enterprise into this context?

THE LECTURER: Fully, but the commitment has to be more than just words. I would like to think that they were committed but I am cynical enough to think that there must also be some rules and laws. We scoffed about seat belts but as soon as the law came in we all started using them. In our heart of hearts we knew it was sensible. My new company is more likely than present companies to act on environmental issues without the law but it would help them if there were a law.

PAUL JERVIS (Bristol Business School): What relationship do you see between the board of trustees and what we call the management or executives? Do you see the board of trustees as part of the board of directors or separate from it and, if separate how does it communicate its sense of mission to the organization as a whole?

THE LECTURER: I see it as a symbiotic relationship. The board of trustees hold the responsibility for the definition of the company's *raison d'être* but clearly it is going to be fed with ideas and wishes by the people who run the company.

ANNE JONES (Department of Employment and Member, RSA Council): How can we enable people to have a better understanding of Japan? We think about it mainly as being competitive and for its technical skill but I have been struck by the philosophy and the social aspects of work there. When I visited Canon, they talked first about their active philosophy and goals, which were to create a harmonious, global, interdependent community. There was nothing about profit and when I asked about it and the shareholders, they said that our shareholders in Britain would have a better chance of surviving long-term if we thought more about strategy and less about short-term profit.

THE LECTURER: We have to find a way of getting companies to understand that they are not just assets to trade on the stock market. The Japanese don't think like that. What impresses me about Japan is they have these statements about values and missions and they all believe them. We have them and nobody pays any attention. They really are immortal communities, and are striving for the good of Japan. To return to

Geoffrey Chandler's point, it would make a lot of difference if more people at the tops of companies stood up and said that was what they were about, that profit was part of it but was a means to an end.

THE CHAIRMAN: Charles Handy's lecture has shown an understanding of the dynamics and the demands of an industrial society and has, I hope, struck chords with those who are in the camp of wealth creation. He has stretched our imagination and challenged us.

SIR AUSTIN PEARCE (Member of RSA Council): One of the very few privileges and pleasures that a Treasurer of the RSA has is to be told that a lecture has been sponsored. Tonight we are triply helped because we have three sponsors: BOC, The Henley Forecasting Centre and Midland Bank and I would like to say a very big thank you to all three of those organizations for deciding that one of the purposes for which they exist is to sponsor events like this one. In one period of my career I was receiving on average sixteen appeals per working day, for money towards sponsorship. Our three co-sponsoring organizations, I am sure, receive even more requests so I am delighted that they have chosen the RSA, and in particular this lecture, as one to which they have so handsomely contributed.

MARK GOYDER (Programme Director, RSA): The RSA's Manufactures and Commerce Committee has already begun to gather together a group of people (some chief executives, some with an academic background) to tackle the questions that Charles Handy raised. Will those interested in joining us in a search for the new shape of the company please contact me so that I can give them more details and make sure they are part of our network?

FIVE

◆

ARE JOBS FOR LIFE
KILLING ENTERPRISE?

My first job was with a large oil company. On top of the pile of
literature given to me on my first day was their pension plan.
Then in my early twenties I tossed it to one side, unread, but I
can still recall my father-in-law-to-be picking it up and
commenting, 'I see that you are worth rather more dead than
alive!'

That, however, was all as it should be because both the
company and I assumed that I had joined them for life and it
was understood that they would be caring for me after
employment and, indeed, after death. They would provide
me with a career, high or low depending on my abilities, and
with the training and development needed to make the most
of those abilities. In return they expected loyalty, commitment
and a certain amount of patience. 'Don't be in such a hurry,
the good jobs come in your forties.'

Life-time employment was the aim of every decent
employer, and indeed of many less decent ones because it did
make life easier to have your own private army to deploy as
you pleased. More recently the Japanese have made it ultra-
respectable corporate behaviour and the paraphernalia of
appraisal schemes, succession plans and career development

officers have welded the idea into every organization's infrastructure.

I suspect, however, that it may be an idea whose time has passed. Even the Japanese, after all, restrict the privilege to their core staff and make it clear that it is only a custom, not a legal right. For they, and others, are beginning to suspect that the disadvantages outweigh the advantages.

The first disadvantage is a simple fact. People grow older at the same rate but organizations narrow towards the top. There is not room for everyone to advance their careers and yet everyone has careers now, not just jobs. The result? A periodic culling of the middle ranks, much unhappiness, and much expense. The culling can only be postponed if the organization's output grows, exponentially, much faster than its productivity improves. That was true for many Japanese firms for several years but is less true now.

It was also true for some British firms but only because their productivity hardly improved at all until the late seventies, which was when the culling really began. Nowadays, every successful firm will have quadrupled its turnover in the last ten years and halved its core staff. The quinquennial cull has become a habit but it makes a cruel mockery of the idea of life-time employment. Half the people, paid twice as much and producing three times as much is a good corporate rule of thumb – except for the other half of the people.

The second disadvantage of life-time employment is the implied need to offer everyone some sort of progression throughout their career. To mean anything there has to be some noticeable advance in seniority, and pay, every few years. That was all right when organizations were big and tall – it is less feasible when they are small and flat. Most organizations are today aiming for four levels of hierarchy.

That does not leave much room for perpetual promotion, or, in hard reality, for any promotion at all for some.

The third disadvantage is that a penchant for growing your own timber leaves you stuck with the saplings your father planted. In a time of massive change the saplings may be the wrong variety. Turning building societies into banks or banks into financial hypermarkets may be good corporate strategy but it is hard to staff the new organizations adequately with the people recruited for the old, train them as much as you may. Inevitably, new talent is brought in, usually near the top and in the middle, making nonsense of the implied promises to earlier staff.

Fourthly, there is the lurking danger of corporate blinkers when the strategy of the business is in the hands of people who have grown up in one world and one tradition and know no other. 'Group-think', as it is called, can make a cohesive group oblivious to anything that they do not want to hear or see, keeping the train running on tracks that lead nowhere.

Frankly, I now believe that life-time employment is bad economics and bad morals. It is bad economics because it puts the organization into a straitjacket and limits its flexibility. It is bad morals because it promises, or appears to promise, what it cannot and will not deliver to more than a few. However well-meant, it is, too often, a lie.

It would, I think, be more honest and more sensible to think in terms of specific jobs with fixed-term contracts of varying lengths, of money purchase pension schemes for all instead of retirement pensions, of 'opportunities' rather than 'planned careers', with people bidding for jobs but sometimes in competition with outsiders. It would be more sensible for individuals to think of 'moving on' rather than always 'moving up', as professionals move from one partnership to another to gain experience or look for richer pickings. Tenure, after all, is something that the good don't need and the bad don't deserve.

What would this mean in practice? The career would become much more the individual's responsibility. I like the phrase that one American corporation uses to describe its philosophy of development: 'individual initiative and corporate support'. Corporate support would include education and training, some of it expressed in the language of individual rights – for example tuition reimbursement schemes, to encourage the individual to invest in his or her future.

Corporate support would include counselling, advice on future job options and appropriate experience. No organization wants to lose its best people and so would sensibly see to it that they are well-positioned to bid for the good jobs; it would, however, be counselling, not planning. Fixed-term renewable contracts would provide the mechanism for periodic discussions on terms and conditions, something that all organizations will need as the individualized contracts of top managers filter down to the middle ranks.

No life-time employment would mean that organizations would increasingly offer jobs, not careers, to people both inside and out. There would be no guarantee that this job would lead to that job or, indeed, to any other job at all. There might be a fixed term put on the job, as we already do for many top jobs, or it might be left indefinite with a notice clause. People would then understand that they were employed to do that job and to do it properly, not as a 'placement' en route to the ultimate 'real' job.

More people might then be around long enough to see the results of their decisions. This would be a nice change from the tradition that really high-potential executives celebrated no anniversaries in the same job. The culture of what my oil company called 'patience' and I dignified with the phrase 'deferred gratifications', or 'heaven later but not now', would give way to a custom which said 'make the most of this job because if you don't it will be your last'. There would be a new sense of urgency and of living in the present.

Many, however, will feel that the abandonment of the concept of life-time employment will leave their business open to exploitation, that they will lose control over their staff, that short-term expediency will dominate personnel decisions instead of long-term development, that the best will leave, that their culture will be eroded and their tradition undermined.

When top managers say such things I am cynical enough to think that maybe life-time employment was always really about control and containment, the easy marshalling of a corps of loyal retainers, and not about the best use of talent.

And did it work even as a means of control? Did not the best sometimes leave? Were personnel decisions never short-term expedients? Were they never held to ransom by great talent about to leave or to enter? Was it not always a bit of a myth?

And then I reflect that the armed services moved to fixed-term contracts in the early fifties when they realized that they needed lots of young talent and relatively few oldies. I reflect that the world of the theatre, of journalism and the media have always worked this way, as have the professions, consultancy firms of all descriptions and, more recently, the money markets. Strangely, or not so strangely, they are all areas in which the British excel – and have they ever been short of talented applicants?

For the best of the British organizations do not depend on

deferred gratification to keep their people loyal. They do it through an immediate commitment to the task and to the philosophy of the business. The best do not need to have been around the same place for 20 years, with 20 years to go to imbibe the culture. In a good organization you can pick up the whiff in minutes. The best know that talent can be spotted, encouraged and given space to grow.

And the best of the British people no longer want to bind themselves to any organization for life, no matter how wonderful or all-embracing it claims to be. These people want to control their own destinies. Their loyalty is something that the organization needs to earn, it cannot be bought by the promise of security. Indeed, to them security lies in their talent, not their contract. They would today be dismayed to find a pension scheme in their joining package. The best want jobs that they can get their teeth into, jobs where the results are the evidence of their worth, not some appraisal scheme – and they want those jobs young. Patience is not in their vocabulary, nor is life-time employment. Perhaps they are right.

CHARLES HANDY

SIX

◆

WHY THERE'S LIFE AFTER WORK

There is a whole new stage of life opening up between the end of full-time employment or full-time parenting and the stage of full retirement that precedes eventual death. Peter Laslett, the Cambridge historian, first gave it the name of the third age to distinguish it from the first age (of growing up), the second age (of full-time work, in a family or in employment) and the final fourth age which we would all want to be as infinitesimal as possible. We need to pay heed to what is happening around us, for demography is a most potent agent of change, all the more potent because it creeps up on us so gradually that we ignore it.

The third age has always existed, of course. It only now needs a word to describe it because it is getting longer and its occupants more numerous. We are leaving full-time employment earlier, with many big firms now looking at an average age of retirement of around 55, and we are living longer and more healthily. The person of 70 today is likely to be as healthy as the person of 50 two generations ago. Before too long, the third age may even begin at 50 and last until 75 at least, an age equivalent to the third quarter of life, perhaps.

One quarter of the whole population will be in this third

quarter of life by the end of the century; one-third of the adult population. They are not dependent, as people in the fourth age are; many will be quite well-off, most will be physically active and healthy; the majority will want to enjoy independence, free from the responsibilities of family and work. So many such people cannot help but have an impact.

The 'young old', for example, are likely to be the next big consumer market. Their money will perhaps be spent on time; time to travel, time to learn, time to practise new skills and enthusiasms, time to relax.

Shopping may once again become a means of social intercourse and not a weekly chore. Patterns of retailing may need to change in response to their new market. Businesses need to plan for this new marketplace.

Health, wealth and a good education are the prerequisites for a good third age. Some will have all three. Many will not. There lies the challenge for society, because unless this third of the adult population is self-supporting, it will become an increasing burden on the generation behind it. Those now entering the third age have been called (by David Thomson in a recent book) the 'welfare generation'. They grew up in a time of heavily subsidised education, housing and health and now look forward to a time of good pensions and good care. They may be disappointed. Their children may be prepared to pay taxes to support the very old, the fourth age, but many will resent the levies necessary to fund the lifestyles of a SAGA generation. It will be better for all concerned if any state pension is bolstered by an occupational pension, by personal savings and by part-time work, the so-called four pillars of life in the third age. Too many will have only one or two pillars if we and they do not start planning now.

The third age is a potential source of labour and of

expertise. But American evidence shows that people are not too keen to go back to full-time work once they have left it. Part-time is another matter. No one likes to feel completely useless. For the managers and the professionals and the skilled technicians, it will be what one might call part-time wisdom work, not energy work; contributing, not running things. As one firm said to a friend of mine, 'we value your experience, Douglas, and your contacts and your knowledge and we want to be able to use them after you leave us, but only on Tuesdays, Douglas, only on Tuesdays.'

For others, the kind of part-time work that Tesco, for example, is offering in some of its supermarkets may be all that they want – a chance to get out and about, some extra money, some socializing, not too much responsibility. What would bore a school-leaver may be a satisfactory part of a portfolio for a third ager and may be the one area in which the surplus of the young old can match the shortage of the young.

'Portfolio' in fact, will be an increasingly useful metaphor to describe the work patterns for people in this third age – bits and pieces of work, some for money, some for free, some for clients or employers, some for oneself. It is, or can be, a most interesting way of living, with little monotony and a lot of flexibility.

The third age will grow in importance. We cannot ignore it. Individuals need to see it as part of life and to prepare for it, financially, psychologically and technically. Organizations must help them and encourage them not to leave it to the last two months. It will make parting easier when people move *on*, not just *out*.

Government, too, needs to make it easier for people to prepare for independence, not dependence. Education, re-skilling and new training need to be easily accessible. The idea of means-tested grants, available to the retired, is one way. Personal savings need more encouragement and personal pension schemes made obligatory, perhaps by requiring employers to contribute to them for *all* workers, including the most casual and most temporary.

The people of the third age, mature, rich in experience, with independence and energy, could be a huge resource to the community. They could also be a burden. It is in all our interest to do what we can to make it an opportunity for all. The people of the coming third age are still, mostly, in their second age and in our organizations. It is there that the awareness has to start. We should no longer kid people that their working life will end when they say goodbye at the office party. We should stop pretending that years of gardening and telly-watching is a satisfactory 'retirement'. We should face facts, see the full-time job as just one phase of life and move on contentedly to the next phase which the French define as the age of 'living'. In my early days at work the pension scheme was rich because on average people lived only 15 months after retirement. There was no life beyond that great organization. There is today. We should be glad.

SEVEN

◆

TEACH YOUR CHILDREN WELL

I was recently given the unusual opportunity to be adviser to a study into the education and development of Arab executives (*The making of Gulf Managers: a study of successful managers in the GCC countries*, by Dr Farid Muna for MEIRC). I know little if anything about Arab executives so it seemed sensible to start by asking some of the best of them how they had been helped to get as far as they had in life, and what had hindered them. Nearly 200 executives were identified by over 50 large organizations as notably successful and those were each interviewed at length and in confidence.

The results were fascinating, partly because what they said is almost certainly true of successful executives in any other culture, including our own.

They listed, in total, ten factors and they ranked them in order of importance. Top of the list came a good education. It was notable that 91% of these executives had a degree or a diploma. It was not the subject of their education that mattered so much, they said, looking back at it now 15 or 20 years later, as the experience, the stretching of their minds, the learning to think, the encounter with new worlds and new people. A comparable study of a similar group of British executives might show that less than 56% of them had a degree or diploma (in 1975 it was 24% of top executives).

Next on the list came exposure to early role models. Parents or relatives or teachers are often the only role models we know. They shape us more than we think. What the father does is always the best predictor of what the son will do. One millionaire executive, an American, was describing his early life to me the other day. 'My father was in insurance,' he said, 'and not particularly successful, but every evening when he came home he would play chess with me, he was a chess fanatic. Now there are two things about chess,' he continued. 'You have to work out the different options and the different possibilities for up to 20 or 30 moves ahead and, most importantly, you cannot blame anyone or anything else for your mistakes. There are no bad cards, no rolls of the dice, no flukey bounces, your success or your failure is all yours. Those things my father taught me with his chess, only now do I appreciate it.'

Third on the list was the experience of early responsibility or the business school of life, as one executive described it. Little jobs and bits of responsibility in one's youth help to build the self-confidence, the willingness to take decisions and to stand the consequences which some people learn too late in life. Entrepreneurs in this country often come from impoverished backgrounds, or have been forced into early responsibility by the death of a parent. The most successful expatriates, another study revealed, are those who have had the most disruption in their youth, and have survived. It is dangerous, it seems, to make life too comfortable for one's young.

Fourthly they listed ethics and values. They were talking about hard work and integrity, loyalty and honesty. Many in the sample mentioned the deep influence of their religion,

Islam in this case, while others cited the example of their families. Others spoke of the importance of having a mission in life, of a search for excellence or for quality in what they do. It is interesting, and reassuring, to see this item so high on the list. It is probably truer than they realized, for what is the point of any learning or development if you have no point to your life?

In their own minds these were the most crucial elements in their success. Yet all of these four elements were already there in place before they ever joined their organizations. Good news for the recruiters, if depressing for the trainers.

Self-development was fifth on the list, by which they meant an active inquiring mind, the urge to seek out opportunities for learning or for study, the willingness to push oneself into new situations, to risk mistakes, to suffer rebukes in the search for experience. All study is an investment, you have to go short of time or money in the hope of future reward; but it can be hard, at times, to give up one's social life or private time. The best of these Arabs did. So do the best of the Japanese. The Japanese in one business once showed me a graph. The bottom axis represented age, or years in the company, the vertical axis the hours or days spent in self-development, for study, or training or just reading. On this graph the line went across and up – the older you were the more you studied. 'It's obvious,' they said. 'Older people have bigger problems and learn slower.' In Britain I sometimes suspect that the line slopes the other way.

Training (nine days per executive per year), technical knowledge, standards and feedback, and formal career development came next on the list – a relief, I think, to the sponsors of the study. Last, but I suspect not least, they listed what one can best call a problem-solving culture, one in which protocol and status are minimized, mistakes are things to learn from, colleagues are allies not competitors, and results are rewarded, directly and openly. Easy to say, of course, and difficult to do but, nevertheless, the very basic ingredients of what people now call a learning organization. (I remember the colleague who said that it was hard to behave that way – he would have been expelled from his school, as a cheat, a cribber and a wet if he had been like that as a boy.) Old habits die hard – organizations like to make sure that no one makes mistakes (and so no one learns), individuals do not always want to share the credit, and status has always been more tax effective to give people than cash – witness all our company cars.

I was reminded of all this by Rosabeth Moss Kanter's new book on the changing corporations of America: *When Giants Learn to Dance*. Her final piece of advice to her corporate leaders is 'have terrific children'. The Arabs persuaded me that the seeds of so much of our future lie with our young people. We should spend more time on them. We should educate far more of them for far longer (only Greece and Portugal are below us on the OECD table of staying on in education of any sort). We should set them better examples and, when they join our corporations, we should give them every opportunity to practise what they are learning, even if they occasionally get it wrong.

EIGHT

◆

WHAT THEY DON'T TEACH YOU AT BUSINESS SCHOOL

I recently attended a gathering of senior executives from a variety of European companies. They were invited to set the agenda for part of the meeting by listing the issues that gave them most concern when they looked at the years ahead for their business.

There was a remarkable unanimity. The new shape of Europe was top of the list, with all its implications for business, new markets, new competitors and new allies. Product liability scored high – would the litigious habits of the American consumers spread to Europe? So did the environment – how far ahead of legal requirements was it wise or prudent for a business to go in its new-found greenery; was there really a commercial advantage in being greener than thou? The Japanese were a perpetual cloud on the horizon for most, but most also accepted that their challenge was no different from that of other competition, just of a higher order.

For some, technology was a concern: how could they run fast enough to stand still in a leap-frogging technological world? Were pre-competitive research collaborations good or bad? Where, if anywhere, was technology and science leading us? Then there were some broad demographic issues. Where were all the bright youngsters going to come from if Olivetti alone could employ all the electronic engineers graduating from all the European universities this year? Would we perpetually steal each other's talent or would we import new talent from the poorer parts of Europe or from India, Asia and Africa? Would that be right? All agreed that women would play a larger role in their firms and that their firms would have to make adjustments to their traditional ways of working if these women were going to be persuaded to join them and to stay with them, but no one was quite sure what these changes would be.

Indeed, some worried that it might be increasingly difficult to keep the really talented of either sex inside the organization. Life on the outside for the good ones was freer and less pressured. Managerial life in the core was exciting and demanding but left too little time or energy for anything else. As one of the executives said: 'my chief concern is me; I want another life and I don't know how to go about it.' Some worried about more mundane matters, such as how anyone was meant to manage the bundle of alliances, joint ventures and minority stakes that now seemed to make up most of their corporations.

This list was particularly interesting to me as I reflected that very few, if any, of their concerns featured on the list of courses at most of the business schools I know. Are the business schools out of touch then? I wondered. Not really, I think, but their focus is different. They are concerned for the most part with those on the lower half of the corporate ladder as they prepare themselves for managerial careers beyond their first specialities. The programmes and courses focus therefore, and rightly, on the inside of the organization or on its immediate concerns such as its customers, suppliers or financiers.

As the executive gets nearer the top, however, their perspective and their worries change. The inside of the organization is at least understood, if not totally manageable, at all times. They would hardly have got so far without being a reasonably competent manager of the things under their control. It is the things outside the organization, the things that are beyond their control, that now become priorities.

It would be nice if there were a business school where you could study all the things which you don't get to study at business school. I once suggested to one of our ancient universities that as it had no faculty that could teach senior managers anything about the detailed affairs of organizations and business, it could turn this problem into an opportunity and help them to examine all the issues beyond the organization, things like international politics, European history, the new scientific thinking, demographics and feminism, even contemporary religion, ethics and philosophy. Managers, I suggested, are generally competent and well-versed in business theory, but so busy in their jobs that their wider education has been neglected, or at best relegated to a hasty skimming of the *Economist*. To put it another way, near the top they need creative, conceptual skills to deal with a whole range of new issues.

Nor will they find the solutions to these issues in any management text book. As Peter Drucker pointed out, the best text on the management of strategic alliances is Churchill's biography of the Duke of Marlborough.

The university was sceptical. It had not been done before. Indeed, but the world has not changed so fast and so furiously before. Much that these executives and their firms would be required to do has not been done before. Little in their past has prepared them for their future. They need to walk in other worlds, meet other people, hear other ideas if they are to cope with the future with free minds. These, after all, are men and women who have lived busy interactive lives. If the research is to be believed, they will not have spent more than ten consecutive minutes alone in the working day. They have not had the time to think, even if they know what to think about and where to start.

The Japanese believe in a reverse learning curve in life – the older we are, the more we need to study, listen and think because the problems get more complex and we get rather slower. The British used to hope that all learning stopped at 16 or at least 21. That attitude is changing at last but we need to find new ways to help people to walk in new worlds before they try to change their own. Perhaps those near the top should go back to university for a term and do all the reading, thinking and talking which they never got round to in their youth. But I would not call them students; in fact I would require them to be teachers and to lead a weekly seminar because, as I know to my cost, the surest way to learn about something is to have to teach it to someone else. Mature students such as these would then benefit any university that had the will to try it.

NINE

◆

A COMPANY POSSESSED?

It is time that we killed the myth; the myth that it is the shareholders who own a business, and that it is for them that we all work. The great majority of shareholders, be they individuals or be they institutions, do not act or think or feel like owners. The pretence that they do not only slants the whole business system in an undesirable way, it also creates an emptiness at the heart of things, the place where a true owner would sit.

Once upon a time those who paid the piper also called the tune, the same people put up the money, ran the business, paid the bills and collected the profits or the losses. It was, perhaps, reasonable to see these principal shareholders as the 'owners' of the business, with the right to determine its future, to sell it or close it down if need be. In a very real way they were locked into the enterprise and were the trustees of its future. The concepts of today's Companies Acts were formed in those times.

Today's times are very different. My dog is mine for life and not just for Christmas, as the car sticker reminds me, but not so my shares. I can and do dispose of them as I please. Most shareholders are like me: traders in company paper, or punters at the corporate races if I am honest. Some others may see themselves as investors, there for the longer term or at least for the first five years of a Business Expansion Scheme.

Some institutional shareholders, too, are so large that, whether they like it or not, they are investors not traders, they are locked in for the duration and inevitably become key players in takeover dramas. The size of their investment means that their interests and their views have to matter in corporate life or death decisions, but few companies think it relevant or necessary to consult them about the more ordinary strategic issues. They are there as investors, as financiers, not as real owners and they have less direct responsibility for the health of the business and its people than I have for my dog.

The rights and powers of these so-called owners are, however, out of line with their responsibilities. Every company is, in effect, up for sale each day, as any chairman knows only too well, and the ultimate power to decide resides with these anonymous outsiders. It is inevitable, therefore, that their numbers transcend all other numbers, that all chief executives spend as much time talking to financial analysts as they do to their staff, that they come to feel it is more important to keep the shareholders happy than the customers and the workers.

That was not, I feel, the way it was ever meant to be. The true purpose of any business is to deliver quality goods and services to increasing numbers of satisfied customers. Profits are a necessary ingredient in that never-ending recipe. I doubt that any shareholder would disagree, but the system forces us to make the profits, and short-term profits at that, the purpose and not the ingredient.

Some people hope that exhortation will revise the priorities. Captains of industry, bankers and ministers all decry short-termism; even those who practise it deplore it, blaming the facts of life. But to cry 'it's not cricket' when it clearly legally is, is only to sound pathetic. If we want to change behaviour then we have to change the rules.

Some would tinker with them, making long-term holdings free of capital gains tax on resale, for example, in the hope of encouraging more investment and less trading. But that might merely result in lazy investors rather than true owners. Others would suggest devices like A and B shares, with only the A shares carrying voting rights (and a proportion of these to be distributed to those who run and work the business). In this case the A shares, the 'owner shares', would probably sell at a discount and the traders in B shares would still call the tune.

I believe, myself, that a more radical re-think is necessary. I believe that the whole concept of owning a company is, today, misplaced. Buildings one can own, or land, or materials, but companies today are much more than these physical things – they are quintessentially collections of people adding value to material things. It is not appropriate to 'own' collections of people. Particularly it is inappropriate for anonymous outsiders to own these far from anonymous people. It is inappropriate, it is distorting, it may even be immoral.

Companies are not, or should not be, possessions to be traded as commodities. They are communities. They need rules of governance, not of ownership. What those rules of governance should be has to be a matter for debate but we ought to look for precedents in the rules worked out for states and communities, not those of chattels. Political and not commercial theory would apply. Powers would need to be appropriate to responsibility, and different lines of accountability would have to be recognized. In addition, it might be thought desirable to make compulsory the separation of powers that actually operate in larger public companies today, with policy (or legislation in political theory) separated from executive management and from an auditing or regulatory function (the judiciary).

It would still, of course, be appropriate for shares in the value of the company to be offered for sale and to be traded on the exchanges. That is how the finance will continue to be organized and paid for. The holders of those shares would be entitled to proper representation in the governance of the business and their dealings would provide a useful financial thermometer of the health of the business – as they do now; but they would no longer be the sole arbiters of its future. Hostile takeovers would, by definition, be impossible since the government of the company would have to give its agreement, but there would clearly be circumstances in which such agreement could be made inevitable, much as it is today.

The best and the biggest of our companies already apply such governance, with careful attention paid to all the stakeholders. There is still no doubt, however, about which stakeholders count in the end – and always more than they ought to. Most of our companies, though, are neither the best nor the brightest. They need the prop of good law, just as it was with seat belts in our cars; good intentions only became habitual practice when a law made it the same for everyone. A little law can change a lot of behaviour, a law of governance, a new Companies Act, could help to fill the vacuum at the heart of many companies and give business back its self-respect.

TEN

◆

Are We All Federalists Now?

Monarchies are out of fashion these days, except for show; dictators all come to a bad end sooner or later; centrally planned economies don't work, even Mikhail Gorbachev says so. Federalism is the thing, say all Europeans, even if the British government begs to disagree, probably misunderstanding the concept or mistrusting its counterparts.

We in business should listen, because the tides which work on the states find their way, in time, to their businesses. Just as citizens are no longer the vassals of some lord, or the militiamen of some warlord (if you will allow me the temporary exception of Iraq and one or two others), so the citizens of our workplaces are no longer hired hands or human resources to be deployed at will but individuals with wills and minds of their own.

Similarly, just as governments find it impossible these days to stand alone in the world and instead need to encompass themselves about with any number of alliances, economic treaties, joint ventures and partnerships, so businesses find that going it alone, however seductive, is too expensive and too risky in many cases. Nearly 700 joint ventures were started in Europe in the last three months of 1989 alone. That is taking no account of the *de facto* partnerships which every firm will have with suppliers, agents, and advisers. Most businesses today are 20/80 firms, with only 20% of all those adding value in some way to the final goods or services actually employed by them.

Similarly, too, just as governments have discovered that it is no longer possible to run everything from the centre – because there are just too many interacting variables – so businesses have realized that the one-time dream of designing organizations like a railway timetable, in which every activity could be pre-planned and pre-coordinated is no longer possible. For one thing it is horrendously expensive. For another, the world does not stand still long enough – by the time the timetable is ready passenger habits have changed, competitors have moved in, the technology has been updated and the whole plan is out of date before it can be implemented.

Businesses, after all, are communities just like any other. They may, and should, have more of a binding common purpose but they are subject to the same pressures, the same unpredictabilities, the same quirks of the human spirit as their larger brethren, the states. We made a bad mistake when we thought of businesses as machines with human parts and started to use the language of engineering to talk about them, instead of the language of committees and political theory.

Take federalism, for instance. It is well that we understand it better since we shall, as businesses, be forced into it, like it or not. Federalism is *not* a classy name for centralization when the centre is in a foreign country. Federalism is a means of linking independent bodies together in a common cause, and since few businesses will be able to, or want to, own all their affiliates or associates, federalism is thrust upon them. A 20/80 firm becomes a *de facto* federation.

Federalism is based, as Jacques Delors endlessly reiterates, on the principle of subsidiarity. I prefer to call it reverse delegation. Subsidiarity is the principle that responsibility and decisions should be pushed as far out and down in the organizations as possible. Subsidiarity is a moral doctrine of the Catholic Church based on the principle that stealing people's decisions is wrong. Put another way, the history of federal bodies is one of independent units coming together and agreeing that the centre can do some things better for them all than they could do on their own, like defence or, perhaps, the treasury function or purchasing in a business. It is reverse delegation. The centre is the residual, doing only what the others cannot do so well.

The language of federalism is interesting and must be used precisely. There is a centre, not a headquarters. The centre does not 'direct' or 'command' but 'co-ordinates' and 'advises'. It is small and relatively invisible, leaving prominence to the local units. Who knows the name of the president of Switzerland or that of the head of Shell International (hugely successful though both are)? In the words of Richard Giordano of BOC, the centre is critic, cheerleader, orchestra conductor and such-like metaphors, using influence more than exerting its power – because how can you possibly use power over those whom you do not own?

To hold the federation together the bits have to be bonded to themselves as well as to the centre. Each should have something the others want and be able to ask for it. Interdependence and a common language would be the principle in political theory. For business the common language is basic English and an all-encompassing information system which allows everyone to talk to everyone at any time. Technology removes the dependence on the centre as a post office and makes federalism a real-time possibility.

Lastly, federations practise the separation of powers. The process of making the laws, or the policies and strategies, is separate from the execution of them and from the regulatory or auditing function. So today, federal firms bring their brains together from around the world to be for a time one organization under one roof, to argue strategies and aims and then go forth to execute what they have jointly determined. Regulation, seeing that the basic rules are kept, is increasingly passing outside the firm to regulatory agencies and auditors. No longer does a small internal board determine policy, execute and inspect. The world, for most of us, is simply too complex today.

Federalism, therefore, is not a rude word. It is an age-old way of linking diversity in pursuit of a common aim. It is, I believe, just one example of how the concepts of political theory are beginning to influence corporate thinking.

There are others, of which more some other time, such as the necessary balance of power and tenure, or the different types of democracy with their advantages and disadvantages, or the rights and obligations of ownership. We are going beyond Machiavelli, one might say.

ELEVEN

◆

ARE THERE BUGS IN OUR OFFICES?

We are in danger, it seems, of making our organizations uninhabitable.

I am not talking about SBS, the 'sick building syndrome', although, as Bruce Lloyd reveals in his recent encyclopaedic analysis *Offices and Office Work: the Coming Revolution*, some 80% of office-workers complain at one time or other of this modern malaise. I am talking of something more subtle but ultimately more deadly. It might be called an organizational work virus – a virus which comes in two varieties.

Last week a personnel director told me that the pervading atmosphere in his organization – a large and well-known one – was that of fear. Not fear of physical violence, but fear of stepping out of line, the fear of making a mistake, of offending the wrong person, of anticipating the boss and anticipating him incorrectly. The most insecure place today, it sometimes seems, is inside a large organization. Who knows for whom the bell will toll if this quarter's results are less than what was budgeted?

The result is a world where eyes are turned down, heads are kept below the parapet and corridors of role-players keep their noses clean. Not the sort of place, said the personnel director, that is going to appeal to the adventurous and talented young, whom, in our strategy reviews, we say we so badly need.

That is one form of the virus. There is another, more seductive but equally dangerous. I invited one of those adventurous talented young to come and have a drink last week. He couldn't make it before eight o'clock, he said; his work group did not even finish for the day until seven – 'at the earliest', his girlfriend chimed in. 'For the last ten weeks he has had no weekends off the job and he is seldom free before nine in the evenings.' It is very challenging and exciting work, claimed the young man, but it was, he admitted, a very unbalanced life and he didn't see how it could continue that way indefinitely.

Both forms of the virus stem from the same cause – the need to improve the productivity of our managerial and staff groups. Manufacturing productivity has improved dramatically in recent years. Now it is the turn of those who work in offices to feel the pressure. Tighter controls and more discipline is one instinctive response; more zealous endeavour and longer hours the other. Both responses aim to have fewer people producing more; both can be dangerous if they are not handled with care.

Leaner, flatter management structures only work if they result in more junior people having some senior responsibilities. The savings come in fewer controllers and requests for permission, fewer inspections and inspectors. More responsibility, however, means that more people will act on their own initiative, and that inevitably means more mistakes. Punish those mistakes, inscribe them in the corporate memory, and you will make it quite certain that no one will exercise their initiative again. The layers of command and checking will build up once more, the savings will vanish.

If the leaner, flatter structures are going to work we have to invest a lot of effort in helping those in the front line to take the right decisions, not in punishing them if they take the wrong ones. Asking for help when in doubt must be seen by everyone as a sign of responsibility, not a symptom of weakness. Mistakes, if they occur, can be a wonderful way to learn, perhaps the only way to learn, as long as we are prepared to admit that they were mistakes and do not try to defend or excuse ourselves. Fear makes all this impossible; fear locks the organization into rigidity, making it conform to yesterday's rules which may not be the right rules for today's problems.

Zealous endeavour and midnight oil, the other side of the coin, sounds more positive. It can be. It can be the infectious enthusiasm of teams of colleagues working on new challenges, aiming for new achievements. There is nothing so infectious and few things more exciting than working in a winning team. Carried to extremes, however, it leads to an almost neurotic obsession with the business. For the business this can mean blinkers and a bad attack of 'group think', the conviction that we know it all, an atmosphere in which doubt has no place, and perspective and objectivity become forgotten values. For the individual it can mean a form of personal short-termism that most will come to rue.

Intoxicating and exciting though such an atmosphere may be, it is not to everyone's taste. Indeed, the more interesting people will fight shy of such greedy organizations because they do not want their lives to be so one-dimensional. There is a particular danger that women will be deterred from entering these companies just when talented mature women may be exactly what they need.

It should not be virtuous to leave holidays untaken, to fly all the red-eye air routes, routinely to work evenings and weekends. Even if we like it that way ourselves it could be folly to make it the pattern for everyone else. We need to look for quality in work and life, as well as quantity. If we don't, we run the risk of our businesses becoming populated only by the second-best. It will not be that the best despise business as an occupation, but that they cannot abide the thought of the organizations of business, consumed by fear and conformity, or else too greedy in their enthusiasm.

TWELVE

◆

IN SEARCH OF AN IDEAL WORLD. . .

'Good evening, sir, may I validate you?'

I bristled at this implication that I was some sort of security risk but the lady in question was only offering to stamp my parking ticket. I was in Los Angeles and must re-learn the language.

It is amazing how well everything works over there. The Avis man checks my car in with a gadget that looks like a personal phone attached to his belt and an itemized receipt comes out of its base, all in less than a minute, just as the advertisements say. The showers are so strong that the water knocks you backwards, the fridges are big enough to sit in, and every home seems to have a kitchen built for a millionaire. This, I am constantly reminded, is a rich country.

It is, however, no longer a country where everyone can be rich. That dream has faded. It is no longer a country bristling with optimism – the place I went to every year or so to get another shot of adrenalin, another surge of enthusiasm, to come back believing that everything was possible if I only tried hard enough.

This time there were too many questions in the air, too much uncertainty, too much fright. Reagan's promise that lower taxes and higher government spending were compatible had proven to be false. The nineties were going to have to pay for the eighties – that, at last, was beginning to be clear. There was fear, too, of another Vietnam in the deserts of the Gulf, and embarrassment that America had to solicit money to pay for its troops, even though it was only fair that the rich everywhere should pay for the world's policeman.

Work too was a worry, and the security that jobs, and only jobs, can buy. Organizations, people had begun to realize with a shock, were no longer the secure harbours they had once seemed – nor was money, or the things that money could buy.

In the eighties, said Lawrence Shames in his book *The Hunger for More* (Times Books, 1989), what counted was what could be counted. BMW cars, condos, Mont Blanc fountain pens, yachts and lavish holidays, these were the signs of success; people came to admire the signs of achievement rather than the achievements that earned them.

Today, there are some Americans who think like the multi-millionaire retailer who said to me, 'so you make all this money, and so what?' The market, for all its virtues, cannot put a price tag on everything. Not everything can be bought off the shelf – not a fulfilling home life, the thrill of reading something new, or having added wisdom to someone else's life, even a stroll by a river on a summer's evening, a talk with friends and a good night's sleep.

A French student at a seminar I gave in America summed it up for me with delightful French simplicity, just touched with arrogance. 'In America,' he said, 'they know how to make things work but they don't know how to live. In France we know how to live but we can't make things that work.' Are the two incompatible?

The hope in America is that there is a new sort of 'more' emerging; that while more money and more success tokens will always be goals enough for many, those people will no longer set the tone of the times. Coming, says Lawrence Shames, is more appreciation of good things beyond the marketplace, more attention to purpose, more determination to choose a life, and not just a lifestyle. Those new indications of 'more' may perhaps create America's new frontier.

Let us hope so – America has always been a pointer to the future. But we do not have to follow slavishly. I do not want a future that encourages you to sue your host for letting you leave his party drunk, or your children's friends' parents if your six-year-old breaks a tooth playing in their garden.

We can, and I think should, borrow from America what is best in their tradition, even if they do not always themselves live up to it. Most importantly, they hold that every man and every woman is born equal and is responsible for their own destiny. We should not feel that we are slotted irretrievably in the background into which we were born and that it is up to someone else to make things better for us. We can and should shape our own ends, rough-hew them how we may, in our organizations as in our lives. Waiting for 'them' to do it, is to wait for Godot; he won't come.

We should go on to borrow from America that erstwhile frontier spirit which holds that there is a new and brighter world yet to be built, that the golden age is not in some distant past but is there just over the horizon if we but walk and work diligently enough. It was, and still could be, a frontier spirit which accepted risks, knew that mistakes would be made, took responsibility, and expected rewards.

To these traditions we, in Europe, can add our own – a sense of history, to begin with, and a different sense of time. As a Czech said to me in 1968: 'We have had many invaders; they always go in the end. These latest are Russians, but they too will leave in time.' They did. Short-termism is not a European tradition. We can add, too, our recognition that not all of us are frontier heroes, that the weak, too, have their place and their contribution, and should be cherished and pro-tected. That includes our parents, our grand parents and, these days, our great-grandparents.

We know too that societies are always remembered in the end for how they spend their money, not for how they earn it. Of course, you have to earn it first, and we have not always been too good at that, but the bottom line is only the beginning. Our organizations would do well to remember that fact, I sometimes feel, just as governments or, indeed, all of us as individuals would.

Europe and America: two traditions, two cultures. We need them both. The hope must be that we can have the best of both. The fear must be for the worst of both.

THIRTEEN

◆

THE PARABLE OF A
FALLEN CITY

Herr Keller is deputy mayor of Dresden in what is now
eastern Germany, not East Germany. He is an engineer who
has spent all his life in a research institute in Dresden. He had
nothing to do with politics until February last year when, in his
mid-life, he decided that the time had come, in his country's
new age, to do what he could to help. He was elected deputy
mayor for a period of four years, and is now responsible for
the regeneration of the city. It is an immense task: to restore
Dresden to its former glory as a beautiful city, known for its
art, music, drama and, of course, its Meissen porcelain.

Dresden was effectively destroyed in one night eight
weeks before the end of World War II by the Allied bombers.
After the war, its new administration pulled down much of
what was left – enlarging, for example, the main boulevard so
that it could take 24 men marching abreast and demolishing
Dresden's only gothic church, which was still standing after
the bombs. Although a few of the beautiful old buildings,
including the opera house, have been rebuilt as they were,
most of the centre is a grey mass, with 40% of the housing in
need of urgent repair and 8% of it completely uninhabitable.
Tall chimneys close to the opera house pump brown smoke

into the air, sulphur from the soft coal smothering the city in a blanket of foul air. The sewage flows untreated into the Elbe, the river in the heart of the city.

The physical problems are the least of his worries. More difficult are the psychological and cultural ones. These are people used to being told what to do, where to live, what to eat and what to believe. Until March last year there had been no proper election since 1932. By a freak of geography Dresden can receive no television signals from the West. They knew, therefore, nothing of the world beyond the wall. It was, Herr Keller reminded me, a centrally planned economy – 'but without the planning,' he added wryly.

Freedom brings choice and, therefore, the responsibility of choosing and of suffering the consequences of choosing wrong. Ownership also brings harsh responsibilities: many of the 40,000 people who rushed to claim the land and buildings that they said were theirs before 1945 abandoned their claims when they discovered what ownership would entail, by way of repairs and maintenance. Freedom means opportunity, but it also means the opportunity to fail. No one in Dresden looks forward to this winter or the next, with all 700 of the city's businesses literally up for sale but many of them, also literally, unsaleable. 'We have to sell companies without selling ourselves,' said the mayor. The waiting list for Trabant cars has fallen from 18 months last year to zero this year. In some businesses this would be called success; in eastern Germany it means that as of 1990 there are no customers for Trabants.

Not surprisingly, not everyone relishes the changes now in train, particularly if they used to sit behind fat desks on top floors and are now out of work or only middle managers for Western firms. Their future is not exciting, just bleak. Herr Keller has had his share of hate mail, his house and garden damaged, he is awash in papers, deputations, decisions – all urgent. He is a quietly modest man who wants to help his city to regain its glory. 'How long will it take?' I asked. 'Thirty to 40 years,' he said. 'How long have you got?' 'I have a four-year term,' he said, and smiled. His salary is minuscule – perhaps £12,000 a year – and Dresden is no longer cheap. If he fails, he will be a marked man, no other job will come his way. If he is thought to be succeeding, he might get his wheel of nails for a further four years. I thought him one of the more quietly courageous men whom I had ever met.

What struck me, as I flew out of Dresden, was that it was a sort of parable for many of our large organizations that have been, if we are honest, centrally planned economies in which most people wait for 'them' to tell them what to do, where to go, how to think; places in which few get news from other organizations of how it works with them; comfortable prisons in which there is little discretion below the top but also little risk.

Today, many of those organizations are unbundling themselves, breaking themselves down into more self-contained units called strategic business units, profit centres, or even separate companies. Responsibility and choice are being pushed out and down. It is all essential if they are to respond faster to a changing world and cut their costs in the centre. They are finding that many of their citizens do not welcome the gifts of responsibility, ownership and accountability, although, as in Dresden, the young and the clever relish the new freedom. Like Dresden, they probably have four years to change the hearts and minds of their people, a job that probably needs a generation. Like Dresden, they will need their Herr Kellers, but I hope they will cherish them more and pay them better. Because, as Herr Keller told me when I asked him why he did it, 'there is today a precious opportunity to shape the future. I cannot ignore it.'

FOURTEEN

◆

SHOULD WE BE PAYING HIGHER TAXES?

I went to an interesting presentation recently. It was concerned with pay scales in Europe and the US. The first slide showed gross salary levels for senior and middle managers. Top of the first division were, predictably, Switzerland, Germany and Austria. The US, surprisingly to me, was in the second division. Britain was low down in the third.

The second slide compared marginal tax rates, the top rates of tax in each country. Once again Switzerland, Austria and Germany were in the first league, joined by Sweden. Britain was again in the third division, this time very low down in it, with almost the lowest tax rates in Europe.

There was a third slide recording the GNP per head of each country. Top of the first division were, yes, Switzerland, Germany and Austria. Bottom of the second division was Britain. It was hard not to suspect that there might be some connection between the slides.

Is it possible, in other words, that the countries in the first division have stumbled on an upward spiral? High gross salaries mean that you can afford to pay high taxes and still live richly. The high taxes can then be used to improve the quality of the infrastructure, particularly transport, telecommunications and, above all, education. The improved quality of the infrastructure makes it possible to get the productivity improvements that justify the high salaries. QED.

Britain has gone for another spiral. On the evidence of the slides it looks as if low taxes allow low salaries and wages that should, ideally, give us cheaper labour costs. But they may, in reality, only encourage higher staffing levels and lower productivity, both made inevitable by the lower quality of education and the poor communications that are all that our low taxes can pay for.

It was not, of course, meant to be that way. Lower tax rates would, it was hoped, encourage people to work harder and longer because they could then keep more of the rewards.

Similarly, those who owned and ran the organizations would realize that they would ultimately make even more profit if they spent some of their profit now on the education and development of their workers. This in its turn would take some of the burden of education off the taxpayer and make it possible to reduce taxes still further.

It was a brave hope but, unfortunately, there is not a shred of reliable evidence to demonstrate that lower tax rates get people working harder. The evidence seems, in fact, to be the other way round. High tax rates make it necessary for us to be extra industrious in order to keep enough to live on. Nobody will refuse a tax cut, for who could resist more money for doing nothing different? But it is gross pay not net pay that motivates. Ask people what they earn and see if anyone tells you their net after-tax salary, or even knows what it is.

Low taxes do, however, act as a 'hygiene' factor. They may not motivate you but they do make the club more attractive to join. Lower marginal rates tempted the rich and the successful back to our shores and made it more worthwhile for the talented to join the enterprise culture. That has to be good news and probably it was an essential first step. Now, however, we need to change spirals. 'Half as many people, paid twice as much, producing three times as much – that's my success formula,' said one chief executive. It's a good formula for Britain too – such firms would, in theory, generate other such firms.

Breaking into the spiral is the hard task. You cannot start by doubling the wages and hoping that the rest will follow, nor will it be popular or effective to start by doubling the tax rates. Perhaps we have to start out at the other end – like eastern Germany where taxes are zero, wages minimal and the physical infrastructure abysmal, but where the qualification structure of an ordinary manufacturing firm reads like a dream. In Jenoptik Gena OmbH, 27.6% of the workforce were graduates, 64.3% were master craftsmen or technically qualified and only 8.1% were 'trained or untrained labour'.

I would not mind betting that the eastern part of Germany will be joining the western part in all those top three divisions before long. If they can, we can. It would not take much to make a dramatic change to our qualification structure – a little money, a little organization and a lot of determination, by both government and business. Give it a decade and we could then start paying better salaries and demanding better work – and might even be prepared to pay some higher taxes to see the spiral work its way upward.

FIFTEEN

◆

THE GREAT ROWING EIGHT OF LIFE

Walking through downtown Tokyo last week I was struck by the number of people wearing white masks over their nose and mouth. 'That's what pollution does for you in what must now be the world's richest city,' I thought. When I mentioned this to some Japanese friends that evening, they laughed. 'They're not trying to keep the pollution out,' they said. 'They're keeping it in. These people are suffering from the current flu epidemic and they don't want to pass their germs on to anyone else.'

It was, in its way, typically Japanese – sensible and thoughtful, a concern for others. Tokyo may be a crowded, stressful place, but it is also a peaceful place, a place without fear of violence. It is also an amazingly punctual place – everyone arrives on the dot and every bus and train departs on the second, usually catching me off balance. It is also a very hard-working place.

'That too is incorrect,' said my friends. 'You read us wrong: we are long-working rather than hard-working. One or two evenings a week we have to spend with our colleagues in bars and restaurants, endless office parties we have to go to, whenever new people move in or out of our department. We are entitled to three weeks' holiday a year but no one ever takes them all, and few people leave their desks in our place until seven or eight in the evening. It's all for the sake of the group, you see, the group is terribly important.'

Yes, I did see, and part of me admired it. The commitment to the group, and beyond it to the organization and beyond that to Japan Inc, is well-known and well-documented, and by all economic measures is astoundingly productive. With it, however, goes the discipline of punctuality, the uniformity (every one of those masks, I noted, was identical as well as spotlessly clean) and, in a way, the tyranny of the group: the peer pressure, the need to conform, the lack of any private space, both physically and psychologically. Some of those aspects I would find hard because they would squeeze out my individuality, my right, even my obligation, to be different. The Japanese don't, most of them, think that to be a problem. Why should I want to be different?

My son recently started drama school in London. Twenty-four of them are selected by the school for an intensive three-year course, all day, every day, with compulsory attendance; just the 24 of them for three years. It came as quite a shock. All his education hitherto had emphasized the individual and individual achievement; now, perforce, it was the group − everybody had to be good at everything, everybody had to get on with and support everyone else because one bad actor ruined every performance for everyone. There could be no solo stars unless all were stars.

Surprisingly, to me, he relished it. Indeed, the group took over his life. He saw no other friends; he spent all his time with the group and even defied illness to get to work with them; he gave up weekends to do extra work or key projects with them and would speak ill of none of them. It was extraordinarily like the Japanese, but I am told that great theatre ensembles have to be that way, as perhaps do all great teams.

I once joked that an English team was like a rowing eight – eight men going backwards without speaking to each other, steered by one person too small to see where they were going! I thought it rather witty until an old oarsman in the audience told me that they would not have the confidence to go backwards without talking if they had not practised endlessly and become totally committed to each other and to their goal. 'You have just defined a great team,' he said. I agreed, shamefacedly.

I have no doubt that all our workplaces could benefit from more of these totally committed rowing eights or theatrical ensembles, these Japanese-style work groups. It would be good for our economy, for our customers, for the people in those groups. But I have my worries. When I was in Japan they were agonizing over their role in the Gulf War and what many felt to be their very belated financial contribution. My friends lamented the lack of strong political leadership and any sense of responsibility for the world at large in spite of being one of the world's richest countries. 'Obsessed with ourselves and progress,' they explained, 'we have forgotten to look where we are going.'

The best way, as so often, must be to have a bit of both, the middle way: tight groups and free individuals; rowing eights for regattas only – not for all of life; individuals who stick their heads above the gang – but do not keep them there; organizations who are committed to a goal – but not a purely selfish one. Just now, the Japanese may need to lean a little towards the British way and think of their duty to the world. Equally, we in Britain could, with advantage, lean their way in our organizations and in our daily lives; after all, apart from those groups, a little more thoughtfulness for others, more courtesy, more attention to the little things, even rather more punctuality and rather less litter, could hardly go amiss.

SIXTEEN

◆

IS THERE TIME TO RAISE OUR STANDARDS?

'What are her standards?' My mother used to ask that question of any new girlfriend I brought home. It used to infuriate me, partly because I did not really know what she was getting at, and partly because I secretly suspected that it was a crucial question, but not one that I was prepared to answer.

Today I find myself increasingly asking the same question of organizations. What are the standards of this place? I say to myself. As ever, I'm not too sure what I mean or what I'm looking for, but I know the answers when I see them, often as soon as I walk into the reception area. They have to do with the way an organization treats people, both those who work for it and those for whom it works – clients or customers. It has to do with energy or the lack of it, with the smiles or the scowls in people's eyes.

More than that, the answers have to do with the point and purpose of the place, with how management and employer see their work and, above all, with their concept of what is good enough. 'I passed, didn't I?' I once said to the headmaster who had complained of my lack of effort. 'Passed, yes,' he said. 'But you failed yourself.' His response zeroed in on the key issue – everyone has standards, but how do you set them and how do you know that they are good enough?

'You British have the misfortune to live on an island,' a German industrialist said to me last month. 'Because you don't leave your island, you don't know how other people live and what kinds of standards other nations expect. You will be destroyed by your insularity.'

He had a point, I had to admit. How many managers have ever bothered to look beyond their nearest competitors, on the basis that what is good enough for them must be good enough for us? It often is, until their cosy complacency is shattered by someone from outside their closed circle who has totally different standards and expectations. 'It's unfair,' the Americans exclaimed when Japanese competition cut swathes through their motor and appliance industries. It wasn't – it was just the application of radically different standards and expectations.

'Help us to be better,' a firm's management said to me once. They were not even clear about which areas they wanted to be better in. 'I cannot help you,' I replied. 'But you will know some people who can. Think of the different organizations you have met whom you admire for some aspect of their work. Go to them, ask them if you can study their methods – none of them are likely to be your competitors. Then come back and apply them to your business.'

They went, they saw and they learnt – but not what they expected. They learnt no new techniques or pieces of electronic wizardry, but discovered instead that some firms expected failure rates up to 100 times better than theirs or had absenteeism levels ten times lower and, in one comparable case, new product development times five times shorter. Standards were different, that was all.

This form of organizational learning has recently acquired a label – benchmarking, the discipline of measuring yourself against best practice in any function or field, often in industries very different from your own. The label, however, reduces to a technique what surely ought to be an engrained habit – to aim to be not just good enough but as good as can be, to look beyond oneself in setting standards for oneself, to shun complacency and the false comforts of talking only to people like oneself.

However, the clearest examples of insularity come today not from Britain but from eastern Europe. In those countries, things and ways and habits of work that have passed muster for more than 40 years are proving to be dreadfully inadequate when exposed to western competition.

Whole industries are closing down, whole communities are out of work when, as far as they knew, they were doing nothing wrong. What they had not done, indeed had not been able to do until it was too late, was to look beyond themselves and measure themselves against other standards. There were, though, compensations in their way of life, they reminded me. When extra work or striving were neither encouraged nor rewarded, most people put their energies into their relationships and the rituals of family and community life. When money was a relatively useless commodity because so much was paid in kind, there was less reason for robbing or prostitution or gambling, or indeed for violence. With western capitalism they may lose the worst of the old only to gain the worst of the new.

Again, I could only agree. Standards are not just about

measures of efficiency, productivity and quality. They are also, surely, about the point and purpose of what we do. As an observer of network organizations, one can only marvel at the Mafia – marvel but not admire. If free enterprise and the market is seen to be a licence to corrupt and exploit, then the West will have betrayed its standards. Capitalism is, or should be, the means to a better life, not an end in itself.

In a lesser way, the post-single-market Britain will face some of the dilemmas of eastern Europe. Unless we raise our standards at work we may lose our standards for life and living. The opportunity lies in the opposite, for if we raise our standards of work, we have, I jingoistically feel, much to offer the emerging European countries in our standards for living. But there is not much time.

SEVENTEEN

◆

WHEN ARITHMETIC DOESN'T COUNT

'If you can't count it, it doesn't count.' It sounds sensible. It was certainly a principle that was drummed into me as I grew up in organizations. It probably explains why there were, at the last count, over 170,000 registered counters in Britain – that is, members of the different accountancy bodies – compared with 20,000 in France, 4,000 in Germany and 7,000 in Japan.

The definitions of 'accountant' differ, of course, in these countries, so the figures are not strictly comparable. Nor do all the 170,000 registered British accountants work in Britain, nor in fact do most of them still practise as accountants – they are our managers. Where the boards of French, German and Italian companies are studded with engineers and scientists, ours are dotted with accountants instead.

Does it matter? Some of my best and cleverest and wisest friends are accountants. Their quality is not at issue. What is at issue is what they count. Accountants were trained, and still largely are, to be auditors first and foremost – society's inspectors, conditioned to look backwards rather than forward, to be cautious in their estimates, to shun risk and to count only what they can put their finger on and cross their hearts about. It is a way of thinking entirely appropriate for auditors, but not always best for the leaders of growing businesses.

They should, instead, be required to count the things that they cannot put their fingers on – the intellectual assets of the company. The market price of most growing and successful businesses stands at a handsome premium to the break-up value of its physical assets. This is no freak of the market but a recognition that things such as brands, research in the pipeline, the know-how of its people, the channels of distribution and supply all have a value which is inadequately described as goodwill. In 1988 Philip Morris paid $12.9bn for Kraft. Less than $2bn of that were assets you could touch and feel. The rest were the 'intangibles'. Arguably, ICI, in drawing attention to the fact that its break-up value was higher than its market value, was inadvertently explaining why it might be a tempting target for any bidder who could release its under-valued intellectual assets.

Second, the counters should be required to count the future as well as the past by recording how the business is planning to develop and exploit those intellectual assets. They should look at how well the future business compares with its competitors, not only in its likely market share but in things like the rate of introduction of new products and services, and by counting the development of intellectual assets as an investment in the same way as they would treat an expansion of plant and machinery.

Because what is not counted doesn't count, there is a serious worry, for example, that there is a built-in bias in British industry against long-term R&D. The consultancy firm SCITEB recently produced an interesting report suggesting that, with the possible exception of the chemical and pharmaceutical sector, the UK stockmarket did not value R&D at all.

Other evidence suggests that the same sort of investor attitudes and percentage figures apply to the investment in human assets more generally. If people are not counted as assets – however much we talk about them as that – but as costs, then there is every incentive to keep down those costs rather than build up those assets. What would happen, one wonders, if our key people had a market price like footballers, payable to the company rather than the individual?

Maybe, too, the new numbers should be a requirement for the annual report rather than for the annual accounts, included as an annexe to those accounts. And to those who would say that any evaluation of the future is a giveaway to competitors, I can only say that this has never seemed to stop firms giving out all this information and more in any prospectus prepared for new capital requirements. If future information is so vital for new investors, why then should it not be required for existing investors?

It is not, however, the investing public that should be our worry so much as the items that concentrate the minds of the board and of the senior managers. As long as these minds are conditioned by the philosophy of the audit, our businesses will inevitably continue to be conservative in their thinking, to undervalue intellectual assets and to count only what account-ants count.

We could, of course, ban accountants from our boards and management offices as they *de facto* do in Germany and Japan. In Britain, however, that would be to jettison the best of our talent. Better by far to change what they count – by law if necessary – and thus the way we all think. Some accountancy bodies, to their credit, are rethinking training requirements. That is for the next generation of directors. My concern is with what is left of this century.

EIGHTEEN

◆

BE GOOD, GET RICH BUT STAY SMALL

Bread, I sometimes think, provides the clue to Europe. No Eurocrat, however rule-obsessed or power-besotted, could legislate the Euro-loaf into existence. By their bread shall ye know them. Bread shops even smell different in each country.

The delight of Europe lies in its differences. Part of the opportunity of Europe is the chance to learn from our different neighbours. It has to be good for us to explore the differences between countries.

It does not stop with bread. Italy, for example, is a puzzle. Here is a country which claims to be richer than Britain, now that they have started to include their black economy in their official statistics. Certainly they all seemed to be living well and healthily this summer with few hints of recession. The only trouble they have is in finding a place in a restaurant for the traditional Sunday lunch.

Yet Italian towns do not bristle with their equivalents of Boots and Dewhurst, W H Smith and Barclays. Hypermarkets are unknown and to each town there is only one small supermarket, the Co-op. Multiples and chains do not exist in Italy, nor department stores nor, with very few exceptions, industrial conglomerates. Families still run Italy, and I don't mean *the* family, the Mafia.

Most Italians have a deep distrust of institutions, which includes large business organizations. They like to keep power close to themselves and to share it only with those that they can, or have to, trust – the members of their family. In Italy you need the family for the connections which get you jobs and for the money which gets you a house – for no mortgage company will lend more than 60% of the value.

Family businesses, therefore, form the backbone of the Italian economy. They are businesses which, like the German *Mittelstand*, grow rich by doing small things well. They will make, for example, the unseen but vital component for the lift in a fork-lift truck or the burners for gas cookers. 'Better not bigger' is their preferred route to wealth because bigger inevitably means the eventual sharing of power with people you cannot know well enough to trust.

Surprisingly, these loose networks of small businesses often seem to manage to produce better goods, more quickly and more cheaply than those from their competitor countries. Somehow they manage without the organizing bureaucracy which we find necessary in Britain, an organizing bureaucracy which may well cost more than the value it adds.

The British will never be Italian. Family businesses are seen by many in the families as traps from which to escape. But maybe there are more fundamental lessons which we can learn from our Italian friends. Clearly, in Italy, you do not have to own everything in order to control or organize it.

Alliances, based on mutual advantage and nothing more, work as well and much more cheaply.

More fundamentally still, perhaps we should question that British liking for institutions or corporations and for organizations with initials instead of names. Maybe they really are the de-personalizing places the Italians think them to be, run by rules rather than by love and trust. Maybe those larger institutions are not as secure or safe as they seem to be, or as productive as they ought to be.

Perhaps we should be more aware of the instrumental fallacy – the danger of treating people as instruments, as tools for the organization's purpose or for society's goals, as cogs for the machine, instead of as individuals with names, individuals who want to make a difference, who want to keep personal control over their lives and futures.

It is this instrumental fallacy which is undermining many British corporations. The best of the young will not have it. They will be individuals not instruments, and the times are moving with them. Rich societies will pay a premium for quality, for service and for things tailor-made. You *can* be small and rich, as long as you are also very good at what you do. The new small bakeries are just one example.

Where bigness is necessary, for R&D, for major capital projects, for global presence, then alliances – from joint ventures to franchising – can work as well or better than a centrally planned organization, even though there can seem to be more hassle in alliances with power so widely spread. After all, the track record of centrally planned operations, be they the USSR or the NHS, has not been all that good.

Britain has always had the largest proportion of large companies (the concentration factor) of any capitalist economy. This seemed the way to a future in which 200 corporations ran the world. This summer in Italy caused me to question this assumption. Maybe the Italians, for all the apparent chaos, know some human truths that we shall ignore at our peril.

NINETEEN

◆

JAPAN'S WOMEN-ORIENTED WORKPLACE

Things are stirring among the workers in Japan. Women are infiltrating the organizations and are casting quizzical glances at the ways they work. So, at least, argued Professor Iwao in a fascinating lecture at the Royal Society for the Encouragement of Arts, Manufactures and Commerce (RSA).

She ought to know. She is a professor of social studies at Keio University, having previously been on the faculty at Harvard. And she had some impressive statistics to show how rapidly the roles of women are changing. No longer is a woman destined to get married at 24 and thereafter be a child minder and home minder for her 'worker bee' husband (her words). Today the average age of marriage for women in Japan is 26 and in Tokyo 31. The average woman has 1.6 children – one of the lowest birth rates in the world – and since there are two-and-a-half million more men than women in the 21–39 age range, women can be very choosy.

Not for them, however, the 16-hour days the men spend working, or rather, she corrected herself, *at work*, for many of those hours are spent socializing, not working. Not for them the 40 years of dedicated more-than-full-time work and then decades of empty retirement with no other interests to occupy their time. 'We have a name for these retired husbands,' she said. 'We call them "wet leaves", you know how it is with wet leaves, they stick around and you can't get rid of them.'

Women today in Japan want a more balanced life. They believe that work can be arranged more flexibly and efficiently. They do not regard the work organization as their tribal community, nor see it as the place which should rank first in all deliberations. They have some more statistics on their side – if the productivity per hour of the average British worker is 100, a recent survey demonstrated, then the productivity per hour of the average Japanese worker would be 60. They just work more hours or, as Professor Iwoa would put it, they are *at work* much longer, take fewer holidays and get home late.

Japanese business, the professor argued, needs women even if it does not always want them. Like all industrialized societies, Japan is short of young people and, particularly, of young, talented people. Women are as well-educated as men these days and there are, in fact, more of them at university. It is nonsensical to use these well-educated people as secretaries or ceremonial tea-ladies and then banish them to their homelands at 24.

Half of Professor Iwao's audience that night were men, British men. She was talking about Japan, but in the first 30 minutes of questions not one man spoke. Clearly what she was saying about Japan had some relevance to Britain.

Traditionally our organizations have been arranged for male convenience. Many of the fashionable management theories have argued for an all-enveloping culture at work. Emulate the Japanese, we are urged, although of course in a suitably muted British way – no company songs or public callisthenics. We have slimmed down our organizations, making them lean if not mean, but in the process we have made them greedy – greedy of our time, voracious in their appetite for our enthusiasms, happy to create a home away from home for high-achieving work addicts. Women are welcome in these worlds provided they share these values; behave like men, in other words.

If Professor Iwao is right, this will not be enough in Japan, and, I suspect, it will not be enough in Britain. Some upside-down thinking will be needed. We have traditionally fitted the people to the work, now we may have to fit the work to the people, as they become our key assets.

One way to do this is to divide the work of the organization into stand-alone tasks, projects or assignments. In some insurance companies, for example, instead of a document being passed from function to function, one case-worker does it all, drawing in expertise as and when needed, and incidentally shortening the process time from 20 days to two hours. A case-worker can be a team or, in the current jargon, a cluster. Not only does this allow the case-worker more discretion about how she or he does the work, it can even allow discretion as to when and where.

If we don't find this flexibility, we run the risk of making our organizations too greedy, of forcing women to choose between career and family, with the possibility that many of them will choose careers and a life which many men have long enjoyed. That could be demographically dangerous. Some of our best will not be breeding or, if they do, will limit it to one child. A reproduction rate of 1.6 per woman will turn Japan into a shrinking geriatric nation within a generation. The sins of the fathers will then truly be visited upon the children, the few that remain to carry the burden.

TWENTY

◆

WORK IS WHERE I HAVE MY MEETINGS

The edges of American cities these days parade their sore thumbs. Tall new office blocks are everywhere, standing tall amidst a sea of car parking space at their base. It's an odd sort of jagged-tooth skyline, made more stark by the fact that both office block and car parks are empty. It's the recession, they say, but many believe that the buildings will still be empty when the recession is long over. We will never again need so much office space, there and here.

'Do you have to work in these conditions?' I asked the lady journalist who was interviewing me for an article in the *Atlanta Journal*. We were sitting in the middle of the huge news room. Nearly 100 people were in there, crowded in front of their screens and keyboards, phones cradled uncomfortably under their chins; smoke, clatter and chatter everywhere. 'No, of course not,' she said. 'I would do most of it much more efficiently and healthily at home but they [pointing to the two news editors behind their glass windows at the end of the room] need us here. Rather, they don't trust me to work where they can't see me!'

Maybe we shall have to break our habit of herding all our people into the same building at the same time to do their work. It will, one day, be quite simply too expensive. Office buildings are the most expensive asset of many a firm; they stand there 168 hours a week, but they are occupied, usually, for only 60 of those hours. Even when the building is open, many of the rooms are empty. Their occupants are not newly redundant, they are out working – meeting clients or suppliers, attending conferences or courses, visiting other locations of the business. For many executives today the office is not much more than a luxurious filing cabinet.

There are some, of course, who must be there, to keep the show going, but for many the office could better be seen as a business club, a place for meetings, formal or informal, for occasional work with specialized equipment, or for appointments with visitors. A club, if one thinks about it, is a place of restricted access, for members only, but once inside there are no private spaces but only spaces for activities – dining, meeting, reading, etc. It would save a lot of rent if we treated chunks of our office requirement as a club – it could even be quite a luxurious club and still save money.

I am told that Mars in the US already operates this way, and that the 42 directors of Honda in Japan share one room, a room in which there are only six desks, because it is assumed that most of the directors at any one time will be out and about, or at home reading and studying. Why should we be different?

Consider some recent survey evidence. One study estimated that over 50% of all jobs in Britain could be done wholly or partly at a distance. Another study, five years ago now, discovered that 23% of British workers would like to work at a distance, coming in to the office one or two days a week perhaps, for the regular meetings and conferences. After all, as another survey revealed, the average office worker in

Europe spends 54% of the time working alone – a figure that is almost exactly the same in both the US and Japan. Why bother to commute in every day when, for half the time, you'll be on your own anyway?

It will not happen quickly. The journalist in Atlanta was right – we like to see our people working. Would it matter, though, if the journalist wrote her copy in the bath at midnight provided she got it in by the 11 am deadline the next day and the quality was up to the required standard?

Fourteen per cent of the British workforce are now self-employed. Not all are exploited homeworkers. Many are independent professionals who work *from* home but not *at* home. If they are clever and lucky they will have a corner in some company's office which they can use from time to time. Others will use the local work centres that are springing up all over. The FI Group even has its own work centres or work clubs where its people go when they want to or when they are needed for a meeting.

Pascal was no doubt right when he said that all our ills spring from the fact that a man cannot sit in a room alone. We all need the camaraderie and the personal contact of the office: a diet of telephones and videoconferencing soon palls if you never meet people face to face; but the camaraderie and the contacts could be for Tuesdays and Thursdays.

We do not have to organize our offices the way we organized our factories. It might be more fun as well as more economic to turn part of those offices into clubs and more of us into club members with our private space elsewhere. Spare then a thought for those developers with their tall blocks waiting for occupants who will never come, or for British Rail with its empty commuter trains – except on Tuesdays and Thursdays, the meeting days.

TWENTY-ONE

◆

HOW TO LEARN FROM THE 'REAL THING'

The Coca-Cola Museum in downtown Atlanta is not, perhaps, the first place that you would think of going to if you were visiting that city, but it is worth a detour for the interested, or even the sceptical, businessman or woman. The museum is, as you might expect, a hymn to the extraordinary success of the strange-tasting brown-coloured liquid that reaches into every corner of the globe.

I suspect that part of Coke's unchanging success lies in the words of one of its early owners, Robert Woodruff. They were quoted to me everywhere I went: 'The world belongs to the discontented.' A constant search for something better, a constant discontent with what one has, a licence to disagree, these things help to keep any complacency at bay. Its Japanese company, I was told, produces and test-markets a new product every two weeks. Even if the vast majority of these products are thrown away, the process keeps the questing spirit alive. Life does not become routine, the past is never allowed to be the only model for the future. It is a healthy discontent. Discontent and, perhaps, the prods of strangers. Of the 5000 headquarters staff in Atlanta, over one-third come from outside America. The group-think which breeds a sort of arrogance, because there is no one around to gainsay accepted wisdom, is less likely when there are outsiders coming and going, questioning and suggesting.

Maybe we should not be surprised at this approach, because these two ingredients are the keys to any sort of learning, and it is only by constant learning and constant re-thinking that we stay alive, be we individuals or businesses. Constant learning, however, is not a very British idea. We are, temperamentally, an L-plate society. The L-plate on our cars means 'learning in progress, please stay well clear, there is an incompetent at the wheel'. That message, too often, lasts for life – a learner is a self-confessed inadequate. Learning, therefore, is something best done secretly, if at all, and best done early on in life.

I do not now remember much of what I learnt at school but the central message, although unintended, was clear: it was that every problem we encountered had already been solved by someone somewhere, that the answer was in the back of the teacher's book and it was our job to find out what it was and remember it. It was a good ten years before I realized that most of the problems we encounter in life are in one way or another new.

I had come up against the difference between convergent and divergent problems. Convergent problems: 'What is the shortest route to Bath?' have only one correct answer. Divergent problems: 'Why do you want to go to Bath?' or even 'Where do you want to go?' have answers that depend on the particular circumstances and which are, in a way, neither right nor wrong. Most business problems are divergent. That is why business is perpetually interesting. It is also the reason why so few of the answers we seek can be learnt in advance, can be copied from books or learnt in school. All that we can do at school is to learn how to learn and then go back to work and practise that learning every day.

Healthy discontent and friendly strangers are, however, only the start of that learning. Space to experiment and the room to fail – for not all experiments succeed – are necessary corollaries. Businesses which continually re-invent themselves give space and authority way down the line and forgive mistakes, provided only that one learns from the mistakes. 'We did not forgive the chap who lent one quarter of our net worth to Brazil – twice!' said one executive. There are, after all, what W L Gore, the textile manufacturer, calls above-the-waterline mistakes and below-the-waterline ones. It is best and safest to learn from the ones above the waterline.

Above all, however, learning needs reflection. Learning is 'experience understood in tranquillity', to misquote Wordsworth.

There is precious little tranquillity in business these days and, therefore, I believe, too little understanding of what has worked or not worked in the past, and of what might work in the future. Professor Alan Mumford has called it 'incidental learning', the learning from the incidents in one's life and work. It has to be organized, this incidental learning, because the time for it does not come naturally; but it could be that this time for reflection, for incidental review, by individuals with their groups, would do more to improve performance than any number of appraisal interviews.

Continuous re-invention, of one's products, one's goals and one's methods, seems to be the best answer to the threat of change, the best recipe for continuity in a time of discontinuity, the best way to ensure a sort of immortality. Who knows, you too might be invited, as Coca-Cola was by Atlanta, to create a museum to your product!

TWENTY-TWO

◆

ANCIENT GREEKS OR MODERN BRITONS?

My Spanish friends are worried about the new Europe, post-1993. On the face of it, their worries are absurd. Spain has flourished since joining the EC six years ago, with a growth rate which averages 5% per annum; and 1992 is certainly Spain's year of celebration – so whence the worries?

Spain, my friends say, used to be an attractive place for international firms to locate their new European manufacturing plants. Labour was cheap but educated. Spain today is no longer cheap. Labour rates are beginning to match the general European standards and the peseta is locked into the ERM and will not readily be devalued. After 1993 every international firm will punch comparative labour and transport costs into its computers and the analysis will reveal that the optimum location for every plant will be along a fat strip from Amsterdam to Milan. They will then gradually close their Spanish plants and move to that mid-European corridor.

Spain, my friends feel, is destined to become the Florida of Europe, a place in the sun for the holiday-makers and the elderly, an economy of service businesses and last-stage assembly. Just like southern Spain at present, they say, the sort of Spain we had hoped to get away from.

Sitting in the sun in Madrid, a visit to the Prado and a fine Rioja wine behind me, I could see little wrong with the thought of a Spanish Florida. But I understood the worries because their concerns apply as much to Britain, also on the geographical fringe of Europe, as they do to Spain. As labour costs level off across Europe, transport costs become critical. The product has to be very good to justify the transport differentials, or very efficiently produced. It will not be enough to be as good as the Germans; we shall have to be significantly better, significantly more reliable, significantly closer to what the customer really wants. Some of our businesses will manage this. Many will not. Europe will then become a challenge which we cannot avoid rather than the opportunity we tend to talk of.

Britain, moreover, does not have the Spanish sun. A European Florida is not an option. What it does have, however, is the English language. Britain, therefore, will be the favoured European location of many Japanese and US manufacturers. The best of them may well be able to help us beat the German standards. If we can only get our transport systems to be quick and cheap and reliable, we should be able to keep those plants in Britain.

The language will also bring us the young of all nations, to learn to speak and write it better. We are destined, willy-nilly, to be the language school of the world. Teaching English as a foreign language is already the fall-back career of every A-level graduate. We can move that business downmarket, unregulated, un-examined, non-standardized. Or we can turn it to our advantage, linking it to our cultural history and turning Britain into the equivalent of ancient Athens, the seat of learning for a modern Europe, the centre of thought and enquiry, the place where every aspiring European wants and needs to have studied at some time.

Britain as the schoolroom of Europe may not be to everyone's taste, but the spin-off benefits could be great. If we do it well we will create, throughout Europe, a fondness for Britain and things British that will bring us customers and partners and friends from all over the Community. It is a role that other countries cannot resent because it will be based on influence not power, a position given to us by others, not demanded by ourselves.

It would require a culture change in Britain, too. Education would need to become a prestige occupation. If we saw it, however, as a business opportunity and not a public-sector obligation, then we might begin to think a little differently, to value teachers more highly, to make our places of learning more like the groves of academe than public lavatories, and to run them more productively instead of leaving them empty for a quarter of the year.

The alternatives are bleak: an off-shore manufacturing subsidiary or a gigantic theme park for tourists, with a fading financial centre.

The Athens option would not only benefit the foreigners. Our own people, too, would reap the rewards of a revitalized and enlarged educational sector. That just might be the ingredient which we need to offset our geographical disadvantage and to exploit the possibilities of the information age and the opportunity to add value through knowledge and ideas. Making learning into an export business could put everyone into business.

In the end, it will be these long-term decisions on transport and the Athens option which will determine our future in Europe, far more than the small print of any treaties or charters. We ought to start thinking about them now.

TWENTY-THREE

◆

THE BIRTH OF THE CONCEPTUAL COLLEGE

Learning is suddenly fashionable. Life is to be a process of continuing learning, we are told, if we are to remain up-to-date in a changing world. Our businesses must become learning organizations if they are to stay competitive. Our schools should, above all, help us to learn to learn as a foundation for life. We ought, the saying goes, to be creating a learning society.

Fine words, no doubt, but one would be forgiven for being little the wiser for hearing them, perhaps even a little puzzled. To be a learner in Britain has never been much of a thing to boast about. 'L' plates are an indication of incompetence, and academic has often seemed to be a term of abuse. Why then, one might ask, this sudden fashion for learning, and what does it mean – more books, more schools, more tests, more exams, or something more profound?

It would be a shame and a disaster if all this learning meant no more than exams and qualifications. Skills and competencies get the job done but they do not describe or define what the job should be. It is all too easy and too tempting to train people beautifully for yesterday's work, and to pay too little heed to creating the work of the future.

Many years ago, Professor Robert Katz, in the *Harvard Business Review*, described the skills needed by the manager. These were technical skills, human skills and conceptual skills. The technical skills could be taught very readily by those who knew them to those who did not. They were the stuff of courses, of books, of exams and apprenticeships. Human skills were more difficult, they could be learnt but not taught, learnt by experience and helped by advice and reflection, what we might call mentoring or coaching.

Conceptual skills were the toughest of all, he thought, and the most necessary because they were the skills that discerned the way, that defined the problems which technical skills could solve, that glimpsed the opportunities and the unsuspected niches. It is no good doing things right – using the technical and human skills – if they are not the right things in the first place. Conceptual skills are what leaders need, the wit to see what needs to be done and the ability to articulate it so that others get excited.

Sadly, Professor Katz had no clues to offer on the development of these crucial conceptual skills. You either had them or you didn't, he ruefully concluded. We need not, however, be quite so pessimistic. Learning by comparison and contrast is one approach, one too much neglected in our specialist age. Our eyes get opened when we see how others do it, compare it with the way we do it, and force ourselves to explain the difference. I understand my own country so much better, Dr Johnson said, when I stand in someone else's. It is too easy for an organization to get so rooted in its own mind-set that it can no longer see itself as others see it. Strong cultures can blinker one.

I was impressed, this summer, by meeting with the seventh edition of the Duke of Edinburgh's Commonwealth

Study Conference. Two hundred and fifty youngish men and women from 32 countries are brought together every six years, this time in Britain, for a series of study visits to businesses and other organizations, in groups of 15, over two weeks. It is learning by contrast and comparison with a vengeance; comparing the 20 or so organizations with each other and with similar organizations back home, contrasting their perspectives and perceptions with those of the other nationalities and personalities in their groups, pushed to explain and comment on the differences to a panel of celebrities, forced to conceptualize their experience.

They will all have gone home seeing their own worlds with new eyes; they will, in short, have had an unusual learning experience that may change their lives.

Learning by contrasts and comparison does not have to be so elaborate or so glamorous. We could all create our own mini study conferences. The Japanese Management Association arranges some 400 overseas study visits in any one year for senior managers. One of the more successful courses at the London Business School required each student group to spend a day in each other's organization and then explain what each could learn from the others. Simple stuff, but even the requirement to explain why you do what you do in the way that you do seems to concentrate the mind wonderfully and get the conceptual juices flowing.

Such devices help to challenge our mind-sets, encourage us to turn our backs on our past, however glorious, and to invent new futures for ourselves. The past has never been a good guide to those futures, but without conceptual skills we seldom had any choice but to go on doing what we did. Now we can, and must, take better charge of our own destinies – and learn the skills which allow us to do it.

TWENTY-FOUR

◆

THE CHALLENGE OF A SECOND LIFETIME

Flat organizations and zero inflation seem to be the things to aim at these days, organizationally and politically.

Both have much to commend them. Ten or more levels in a hierarchy has always seemed to be more to do with a pecking order than with operational efficiency and it would be nice, would it not, to get back to the days when money kept its value for a century or more, as it used to do. But good news always comes with side-effects.

Should these two *desiderata* come to pass, we will need to reconsider all the reward and compensation systems in our organizations. It is already beginning. Promotion every two or three years as recognition of achievement is no longer possible when the ladder has only got four rungs. Annual across-the-board increments are unnecessary when inflation is zero. Perks such as cheap housing loans mean little when people stop buying as a hedge against inflation and go back to renting as they always used to do. If income tax continues to come down, to be replaced no doubt with a variety of expenditure taxes, then other tax-reducing perks will also lose their bite.

Level playing-fields are great in theory, it seems, but if you were skilled at exploiting the distortions in the old ones, the new fields can be uncomfortable for a while, requiring fresh tactics and different approaches. If promotions, perks and percentage increases no longer work so well, how can organizations best reward effort and achievements and provide incentive?

The challenge could be healthy. Instead of congratulating someone on their success by removing them to a new job, we shall need to encourage them to do the same thing better.

Profit-sharing and performance-related pay are therefore becoming increasingly common in businesses as they move to flatter hierarchies. Typically, someone will soon receive an annual pay packet made up of four parts – a basic rate for the job, a share of the corporate profit, a share in the group bonus and a personal bonus for personal performance. All these last three elements will vary, of course, from year to year and will not become part of the next year's base rate. High pay will always, therefore, have to come from higher productivity, and collective bargaining will be restricted to negotiating the rates for different skill levels. To reduce the arbitrary nature of this largesse, some businesses guarantee that a fixed percentage of their annual added value will be available for the various forms of performance-related rewards.

It might get even more interesting. The bonus could come in the form of extra holidays, in educational opportunities or in travel. The chance to choose might be a bonus in itself.

Doing the same thing better can, nevertheless, get boring. 'I have been looking into people's mouths for the last 40 years,' said a dentist friend, 'and I can't do it one day longer.' Copy, then, the Japanese who have developed what I can best call the horizontal fast-track. They make sure that the best of the brightest switch from project to project and, in their youth, from speciality to speciality. New teams and projects provide new challenges for high achievers. Projects can get successively bigger – a form of promotion through task in place of promotion through the hierarchy.

Put performance-related pay and promotion through task together and the result can be significant rewards for significant achievements. But one's performance does not necessarily improve continuously and forever. Organizations must contemplate the reality that individuals will be assigned to less significant projects, that total pay can decrease as well as increase, and that a person is only as good as his or her last two or three assignments.

We may, in fact, be seeing the end of the life-time career contract, or at least the undeclared presumption that there will be a role for one up to retirement. The reality is that few, these days, reach the official retirement age. It might be more honest and more healthy to introduce a series of fixed-term contracts, renewable and renegotiable, rather as the British Army does. We already do it for many of our senior executives. The practice could and maybe should spread downwards.

If renewable fixed-term contracts become more common, more people would think of and plan a second career 'beyond the job'. The organization will, then, become just another part of life's journey, not the bulk of it, and not always or necessarily the best part.

With luck and good management, the combination of flat organizations and zero inflation may result in second careers for all of us, more open and honest organizations with more attention paid to the task and less to the pecking order. Good news for the competent; bad news, I suspect, for life's passengers.

TWENTY-FIVE

◆

FLEXING, CHUNKING AND CHANGING

It is time to rethink time.

For generations, and certainly for all of this century, our time has been arranged in a set and rarely changing tradition. Men went to work from Monday to Friday, from nine to five and sometimes on Saturdays. Women worked longer but a lot of it was at home. There was overtime and there were shifts but these were extra or special and paid accordingly. There were two, now five, weeks of holiday every year and eight days which are still mysteriously called Bank Holidays. Men retired at 65 and women at 60 and, supposedly lived quietly on their pensions until they died. Schools and colleges had long summer holidays to help with the harvest and to allow their teachers to recuperate and refresh their brains. Sundays were non-trading days unless you were, strangely, a garden centre or an off-licence. We all knew what was when and who was where.

Today it is all changing. Wandsworth schools will soon move to five eight-week terms a year. Stores stay open until 9pm or 10pm and on Sundays. Financial offices keep Tokyo and New York time as well as London time. Factories of all sorts work around the clock, like process plants, or, come to think of it, as hospitals, prisons, parts of airlines and railways and postal services have always done. It is as if we have suddenly realized that there are 168 hours in the week, not 40, and that assets do not have to sleep just because humans do. The implications, however, for those humans who have to sleep are huge.

Everyone everywhere is therefore beginning to re-chunk their time, from choice or necessity. Some are cramming a lifetime's work into 30 years of 65-hour weeks, postponing most of their leisure until their third age. Others would love to have that opportunity as they find that they are expected to take all their leisure now and call it unemployment. More and more people are selling bits and pieces of their time to organizations or customers, as part-timers or independents, and apparently are mostly liking it that way. Nine out of ten of the six million part-timers, who make up one-quarter of the workforce these days, say they do not want a full-time job. It is true that they are usually the second earners in a household, which is another way of saying that most of them are women but, apparently, one-third of all full-timers would also like to work part-time at some stage in their careers. Time can, at times, be more valuable than money. To put it another way, most of us would like to have more control over our time. So would organizations, as they increasingly export their uncertainty into the workforce. The stage looks set for a clash, but it just might be that the new flexibilities could work to everyone's advantage if we take thought and take care.

In an important new book, *About Time*, Patricia Hewitt sets out all the numbers and also provides a long list of all the new ways of chunking time or arranging work schedules in organizations. There is, of course, flexitime, and the pressures for a 35-hour week. That could mean an hour off each working day, *or* Friday afternoons off, *or* a nine-day fortnight. There is part-time working for new parents, part-time before retirement, job-sharing, term-time jobs, weekend jobs, four ten-hour days a week or eight-day fortnights, annual hours contracts, zero-hour contracts (being available to work as and when required), parental leave, career breaks, sabbaticals, time-banking (accumulating holiday entitlements over several years), and individual hour contracts where individuals and their bosses agree on a timetable of hours each month or week.

More different kinds of chunks to play with, more individual choice, more organizational flexibility – on the face of it there could be good news for everyone. Inevitably it is not that simple. Men and women, critically, have different life/work cycles. Women cannot easily combine those 65-hour weeks in the core with family responsibilities. When they can once again manage those hours they are often told that they are too old (at 40?) or out of touch. Men often like the hours if they have family responsibilities, because their earnings increase, but would like to ease off later on. Ironically, if we chunk the core jobs so thickly and so indiscriminately we may be excluding many of the best and most talented of our people, given that half of all our graduates are now women. We need to make those core jobs more time-flexible by, for example, allowing people to spend part of the day or the week working from home, by concentrating on results and not worrying too much about where or when the work was done as long as it was on time and up to standard, or by making it easier to move from core jobs to portfolios and back again.

Portfolios, the idea that one's work is a portfolio or collection of projects, clients or products, whose mix varies over time, are becoming an increasing career option as more and more people work outside the organization by choice or force of circumstances. Already only 55% of the total potential workforce, a definition which includes those wanting work but without it, have full-time jobs inside an organization. It is a percentage which is likely to go on falling as organizations slim down to their essentials – recession or no recession. Indeed, if you add in all those adults of working age who are working, but not paid because they are busy caring for their homes or relatives, the majority of us are now living portfolio lives. The full-time worker is now in a minority. In fact, as Hewitt shows, the nine to five pattern, give or take an hour or two at each end, now only applies to one-third of British workers. Time at work is not what it used to be, nor, I reckon, will it ever be again.

We need, therefore, to think more imaginatively and positively about how we chunk our time, both as individuals and as organizations. It can be revealing. As a portfolio worker I re-arranged my own time a few years ago. I allocated 125 days to administration and teaching, and 100 days to researching and writing, the ways in which I earn money. I added on 25 days for so-called 'gift work', the time which I give to my causes, enthusiasms and occasional good works. That left 115 days for leisure, holidays and family. 'What a nice leisurely life you lead!' said a friend. 'I suppose that's the bonus of being some sort of writer!' I asked him to add up his own 52 × two weekend days, his eight statutory bank holidays and his 25 working days of annual holiday and watched his face as he realized that he, like most so-called full-time workers, had 137 leisure days a year if he chose to use them.

We need, however, to recognize the realities of the new workforce, one in which not everyone will be able to fill 225 days with profitable work. If the majority of us are outside the organization, where then will we be trained? How will we build up our pensions? What will happen if we get sick? Will we be able to have holidays? Who will help us negotiate our rates or our hours? If governments think that these questions will all go away once the recession ends they are mistaken. The new minimalist organization is here to stay. If they think that it does not matter because an outsider workforce means a cheaper workforce which means a more competitive Britain, then they are in danger of mortgaging our children's futures. And if they think that we are all responsible enough and far-sighted enough to train ourselves and fund ourselves and pace ourselves, then they overestimate most of us.

We have now got the chance to shape our time to suit our needs and to flex that time in different ways at different stages of our lives. Our grandparents never had that chance. We would be crazy to throw it away because we failed to notice it, or thought that it would take care of itself.

TWENTY-SIX

◆

PAYING OUR LAST RESPECTS TO HONOUR

Within days of taking the presidential oath of office in January, Bill Clinton had lost his prospective attorney-general. Zoe Baird, who was widely admired for her talents and a very visible symbol of Clinton's equal opportunity commitment, had resigned.

What had she done? She had knowingly employed two illegal immigrants to help run her home. The misdemeanour, however, was not the whole point – it was her attitude to it. It was, she admitted, technically wrong, but ought not to be the sort of thing to debar her from office. Everyone does it, she seemed to think, and everyone knows that everyone does it, so it cannot really be wrong. She had failed the judgment test. Not only had she blurred right and wrong, but she seemed to think that those who are called to great things should have more forgiven them than lesser mortals because they have more to offer. It sounded indecently arrogant.

Clinton was right not to try to defend her. Democracies are built upon respect, respect for laws and institutions and for those who inhabit them. There are, unfortunately, no watertight compartments in high places. Lose respect in one part of your life and the loss rapidly spills over into all the other parts. Like a pane of glass, respect, once cracked, cannot be put together again in quite the same way.

The chairman of a North American company was telling me of his alliance with a Japanese telephone company. The Japanese made the phone, the Americans made the battery. Their new product had only just been launched when they heard, in North America, that one of the phones had blown up beside the ear of a Japanese gentleman. 'We went into emergency session with our lawyers,' he said, 'and waited for the writs, but nothing came. After a week we tentatively peered over our parapet and rang our associates in Japan. "Tell us the worst," we said, "who is suing whom and for how much?" "Oh, no problem, no suing," they replied. "Our president went at once to the hospital, offered his apologies and his resignation, matter is closed." If we did that over here,' the North American went on, 'we should be admitting our legal liability and would be laying ourselves open to massive damages.' So, no apologies, no offers of resignation.

It is a consequence of their, and our, legal tradition. Never explain, never apologize, we say. Above all, do not resign, even if the whole world knows what happened. Let them snigger, let them gossip behind your back, let unfounded rumours spread, it is all better than admitting to a mistake and accepting the consequences. Besides, we are, each of us, too valuable to be sacrificed on the altar of peccadilloes. I wonder, however, if it is better, because the one consequence you cannot avoid is the loss of respect, the respect of those who work with and for you, the respect of your customers, the respect of the general public.

When GM's pioneering Saturn corporation discovered a flaw in the fuel system of their new model, they did not recall the 12,000 autos already sold, they sent a brand new car to the astonished owners in return for the flawed one. Result? Enhanced respect all round and 12,000 Saturn enthusiasts.

Honesty often pays. Genuine apologies, not the British Airways sort which come with a directorial disclaimer of any involvement, but quick and sincere apologies, along with generous reimbursement, are well-known to win loyalty. The best way to win devoted customers, it sometimes seems, is to do them wrong, then do them right in trumps!

I suspect that I am not alone in thinking that the Zoe Baird syndrome is spreading in high places, the syndrome which holds that trivial misdemeanours should be forgiven to valuable people and to important institutions. I suspect that I am not alone in finding myself commenting more often of more top people that if they did know that skulduggery was going on they should have stopped it, and that if they did not know, they should have known. I suspect that I am not alone in lamenting the passing of a sense of honour and of obligation.

These are not the nostalgic yearnings of an ageing bystander. I know how difficult it is in a stressful busy life to do nothing wrong or shameful, often by omission. Few of us would survive the scrutiny meted out to potential holders of high office in the US. Yet a society without respect for its leaders is a society ready to disintegrate. These days, many of our institutions, the law, the city, the monarchy, the government and business itself, are regarded with diminishing respect, partly because some of those who lead them do not themselves command respect. The Zoe Baird syndrome feeds on itself. If they behave like that, given who they are, then it must be all right for us to do likewise. The downward spiral has started.

TWENTY-SEVEN

◆

CAN THE DREAM BECOME A NIGHTMARE?

Shenzhen City is the heart of one of China's special economic zones, her attempt to demonstrate that socialism and open-market capitalism can co-exist. Fifteen years ago it was a village amid the padi fields. Now it is a city the size of Bristol, with apartment blocks rising into the sky, all the mirrored-glass skyscrapers you could wish for, tree-lined boulevards and traffic jams. They say its industrial output increased by 40% last year but I doubt that anything stood still long enough to be counted.

Guandong, the province, has a population the size of Britain and has been growing its economy at 14% for the last decade. The 80 miles of road from Guanzhou, the capital, to Shenzhen City, is one long building site. Everywhere there is dirt, mess and scurrying activity, hundreds and even thousands of people busy creating myriad forms of wealth. Multiply all this by 20 and you get some idea of China's potential if the Guandong experience is allowed to replicate itself throughout the country.

It is a little quieter in Kuala Lumpur, but not much, and it is certainly more tidy. I lived there 30 years ago and my return there was a trip down memory lane. Memory Lane had become an eight-lane highway, buzzing with Mercedes and lined with flowers. The Malaysians are planning on a modest 7.2% growth per annum over the next 30 years, which will bring them up to today's US standard of living by the year 2020. There seems no reason to suppose that they won't do it.

Singapore, that Intelligent Nation Corporation, as it likes to call itself, has no doubts that it will get there. 'The Next Lap', its new plan, explains how. Indonesia is starting farther back, with 60% of her population still on the land, but it is the fourth largest country in the world, in terms of population, as they kept reminding me, and they want to be one of the greatest. Add to these countries Taiwan and South Korea and, of course, Hong Kong, and the tigers of the region are really showing their paces.

It is exhilarating to stand in the streets of these cities. If you think that 8% growth is normal, you do things, you take risks, you move, in ways unthinkable in lands like ours where 3% is a rate of growth we can only hope for. In 8% lands, let alone 14% ones, if a building doesn't work you pull it down and build another. Nothing seems impossible or too big.

They realize, all these countries, that their real competitive weapon is the minds and hearts of their people. The old sources of wealth – natural resources, technology and capital – are now available to anyone who can buy them. The only thing which counts now is the process skill of the people, the ability to harness the resources which you have bought. Bringing the minds of the people up to scratch requires an investment of something like 20% of GDP in education and training. Coasting along, as we do in Britain, at perhaps 12% of GDP will not be good enough.

Then there are the hearts. Malaysia has its Vision 2020, a dream of a nation which they are determined to turn into reality. The 7.2% growth rate is just the fuel for it. They want a land of greater equality, of more comfortable living, of better deals for the handicapped, of freer hospitals and easier old age – all spelt out in terms of goals. I expected cynicism, even mockery, from the business community for this national 'mission statement'. Instead I found admiration and commitment even though the delivery would require initial sacrifice all round. It was the same everywhere. These countries each have a dream, and it makes a difference. Asked if we had a dream, I could only offer Maastricht.

Malaysia's dream, however, was multi-faceted. The others did not get beyond the economics. That worried me. What were the economics for? The real dream of so many seemed to be encapsulated by Pacific Place in Hong Kong, a gleaming marble shopping plaza, dripping with Gucci and Ferragamo. Consumption and conspicuous expenditure seemed to be the sought-after goal of all the frenzied activity. But consumption, we could have told them, does not in itself bring happiness.

Societies have always been remembered by history for how they spent their money, not for how they earned it. We, in Britain, run the risk of leaving no remembrance of these times because we will not earn enough to start with, if we choose not to invest in the minds of our people. The tigers of south-east Asia may be remembered only for their glass towers, their shopping malls and their traffic jams. We, and they, need our own Vision 2000.

Without such a unifying vision, selfishness is licensed, corruption can run riot. What started out as a natural desire for good things could easily end in misery. We in Europe have seen it before and are seeing it again. They have as much to learn from us as we from them.

TWENTY-EIGHT

◆

WHEN COMPANIES ARE CONDOMINIUMS

The statement 'our people are our greatest asset' might just be beginning to be literally true, with consequences which are unforeseeable.

Last year, for a short time, the market value of Microsoft overtook that of General Motors. The *New York Times* commented that the only real asset possessed by Microsoft was the imagination of its workers. Tom Peters was moved to proclaim the symbolic end of the industrial age. Peter Drucker, in his latest book, *Post Capitalist Society*, pointed out that the 'means of production', the traditional basis of capitalism, was now literally in the heads and hands of the workers. What Marx once dreamed of has happened, though not in a way he could ever have imagined.

It turns capitalism on its head. Traditionally, those with the money have owned the means of production and have then hired people to put those means to work. Our financial statements, our stock markets and, most crucially, the structures of our enterprises have reflected that tradition. Financiers own and dispose of their property, their assets; they create institutions where lives and livelihood depend on the development and exploitation of what they own. But you cannot own people's brains. You cannot, in a democratic society, prevent them from taking those brains elsewhere. You no longer control your assets as you used to do. The assets own themselves.

People assets, therefore, present us with a paradox. If our people are our ultimate competitive advantage, as they are, we must invest in them, develop them and give them scope for their talents. The more we do that, however, the more we thereby enrich their passports and increase their potential mobility. There is, however no escape from the paradox because we cannot afford not to invest in these new mobile assets. You can already sense the change in our corporate cultures. Decades ago, I started life in an international oil company of high repute. They accepted responsibility for my life, even beyond retirement. In return, I remember, I thought it only reasonable that my appraisal should score me on 'loyalty'. That word no longer appears on the company's appraisal forms. Loyalty is now first to one's own professional development, to one's own career; second to the current project, team or assignment, and only third to the institution where that career or assignment is currently lodged. Love yourself, it seems, then your neighbour and then your corporation, in that order.

Nowadays the organization cannot demand the loyalty of its people: it has, instead, to earn their loyalty. There is no logical or economic reason why those assets should not go to a better hole if they can find it. One should perhaps beware of those who swear undying loyalty; it may be that they have no other hole to go to. As my boss once said to me when I told him of a tempting offer from a rival for my services: 'We expect our best people to be wanted by others, we just hope that they won't be persuaded, and certainly not by mere money.' This is the newest challenge to leadership – to make your hole the preferred hole for the best people.

My guess is that the growing importance of people assets will turn more and more corporations into networks of project groups, a sort of corporate condominium, collections of temporary inhabitants clustered together for mutual convenience, for a time. There will be good news and bad news in this. It will keep organizations and individuals on their toes, innovation and creativity will be essential, people will want to invest in their own futures and not leave them in the hands of their superiors.

On the other hand, corporate empires will crumble and, with them, will go much of the long-term thinking, the career structures, the ground-rules and the traditions. To what do we really belong if we are only the members of an exciting project team which may not be there next year? How will investors know what their shares are truly worth when those shares depend on a shifting mix of projects staffed by mobile brains?

My hope is that the new 'corporate condominiums' will be far more than temporary coalitions of hired brains, that they will develop standards and a way of life; that they will be mini-states where one is proud to be a citizen, rather than temporary parking lots for our talents. If, however, we are going to treat our people as citizens rather than as hired help, then we shall need to give them the rights of citizenship, which may include some of the rights which previously went with ownership. If we start to do that, then we may see a new development of capitalism. If we change nothing then we shall, I fear, degenerate into a culture of temporariness, of selfishness and opportunism. It will be fine for a few for a time, but bad for most.

TWENTY-NINE

◆

MAKE YOUR BUSINESS A MONASTERY

I have always disliked the term 'voluntary organization' and its even worse equivalent – 'non-profit organization'. Neither of the terms are correct. Most of the people who work in the big charities are no more volunteers than someone working for BP or BT. They are paid staff, there because they want to be there, it is true, but that is equally true, one hopes, of the executives in BP and BT. As for profit, while they may not distribute it, these organizations are as anxious as any to make an operating surplus.

Nowadays I like to call them 'social businesses' because they are businesses in most senses of that word. They are concerned to turn inputs into outputs as efficiently as possible for the benefit of their clients – not a bad definition for any business. Of course, those benefits are social benefits of one sort or another and they don't have the dividend pressure but, otherwise, there should be little difference. Realizing this, the social businesses are increasingly turning to commercial businesses and commercial consultancies for help and advice.

They have much to learn. Not least, they often need to discover more about the proper definition of roles and responsibilities and the art of sensible delegation, so that they can run their businesses without the endless meetings that are the bane of this sector. This, however, is not a plea for more unpaid consultancy, but a story of how I have often learnt more from them about management and business than they have ever learnt from me.

I have learnt, for example, that to work for a cause can be wonderfully exciting, much more exciting than working for the shareholders. Not so long ago I attended an unusual executive seminar run by an international hotel chain. It was unusual in that the opening presentation was given by a Benedictine monk from a monastery in Provence. His theme was hospitality. His monastery, he explained, was a sort of hotel. All sorts of people dropped in for a few days of quiet and reflection. He and his colleagues welcomed them all in the spirit of St Benedict who, the monk explained, had a rule of hospitality. We must welcome, he had said, every man, each man and the whole man. For 'man' these days, the monk was careful to explain, they now meant man and woman. By 'every man' St Benedict meant that they were to make no distinction between president and pauper, and they had actually received both in the last month in Provence. By 'each man' was meant that they were each to be treated as individuals, not slotted into categories. By the 'whole man' St Benedict wanted to make sure that visitors were not treated superficially but that their deeper needs were met, that they should have opportunities to explore themselves and their surroundings as far as they wanted to. It was, he said, wonderful to see them leave 'renewed'.

The monk's talk was received rapturously. Their hotels, you could see them thinking, could be like his monastery. He had made hotel-keeping into a mission, a social business. It was a hard douche of reality to check into one of their hotels later that day and find that every movable item was chained to the wall, that even the loo roll was in a locked metal container. 'But we have to,' the manager later explained to me. 'Some of these visitors, they steal everything they can get their hands on; our profitability would vanish if we left things loose.'

The social business ethos was well captured by George Bernard Shaw, in *Man and Superman*: 'This is the true joy in life, the being used for a purpose recognized by yourself as a mighty one; the being a force of nature instead of a feverish selfish little clod of ailments and grievances, complaining that the world will not devote itself to making you happy.' The social businesses, even the most muddled of them, know the truth of this. The sense of being used for a mighty purpose makes up for their small inefficiencies, their often lousy pay and poor conditions. You have to experience it to know what a difference it can make, to have such a cause.

Keeping the shareholders happy is a primary obligation of any commercial business. We neglect it at our peril. But it hardly ranks as a cause. Elevating it to a passion, making them indecently rich, doesn't help, unless you are one of the shareholders. We have to find something else. I suspect that the executives in that hotel chain will now try to instil in their people a bit of the Benedictine vision of hospitality, to make it respectable in their business to find delight in taking trouble to make their visitors purr with pleasure. Maybe next time I go to one of their establishments, instead of being seen as a 'clod of grievances' and a potential thief in the night, I might sense a real pleasure in my presence.

THIRTY

◆

WHAT IT TAKES TO MAKE A MANAGER

Earlier this year I gave up my title of Visiting Professor at the business school which I first joined more than 25 years ago. A business school then was a new phenomenon. 'Why such excitement about a typing school?' a friend asked me. Now they are everywhere. At that time I thought that there was a science of management which, once it was known and taught, would solve all our problems. Now I know better. I know, for instance, that you can know everything that there is to know about business and still be a lousy manager.

Twenty-five years ago, what business education that there was mainly consisted of two-day events. The long graduate programmes at the new London and Manchester Schools were just starting, but if anyone boasted of that strange degree, an MBA, he or she must have got it expensively in the US.

Today there are over 100 degree courses in business and management in the UK, and a myriad of other courses without degrees attached to them. An MBA is no longer a licence to name your own salary but is increasingly a starter kit required of aspiring executives in a wide range of occupations. That is as it should be.

If we took a more realistic and broader view of education

in this country, we might not need business degrees at all. That is not because business education is unnecessary but because it is hard to see how anybody can get on without it. These courses provide the grounding in economics, statistics and applied psychology that any working person needs, together with the more vocational introduction to finance, marketing and interpersonal skills. 'How do people get by without knowing the difference between full and marginal costs?' my teenage son asked in wonderment after his first introduction to economics. 'Not very well,' was the only answer I could give.

Over and above these useful bits of knowledge and understanding, a good business course will teach you to think strategically, that is, to work out where it is you want to go, and what you will need to do in order to get there. I could, therefore, make out a good case for requiring a business course to be part of the last year of schooling for everyone, or at least the first year of any university course. To have rationed all this useful education, to have offered it at premium prices to a fortunate few, and then to give it the dignity of a postgraduate degree and let the students think that they were now professionally qualified managers was, I can now see with hindsight, an unfortunate mistake.

It meant, for instance, that people expected things from these courses, and from those who went on them, which no course could realistically deliver. I used to tell those who were interviewing the applicants for one such course that they should look out, initially, for those who, in one sense, did not need to come. I meant that we needed students who already showed signs of the management qualities which we could not teach; things like perspicacity, ambition and tenacity, the ability to be both tough and tender, to be able to work with people and to handle power but with responsibility, to have, even, some charm and a sense of humour. We could then add the science of analytical thinking and some necessary knowledge and skills.

That remains true today. Courses can help people to think more clearly, but they cannot change their behaviour or their personalities or most of their values.

Business studies are becoming a prerequisite for many careers, something which every individual would be wise to do as early as may be. Learning to manage, however, is something else again, something more particular to each situation and, I now think, to each individual.

Looking back now, over those 25 years, I am amazed that I ever thought that there could be one universal theory of management, waiting for us to uncover it by diligent research. We all need a starter-kit of knowledge and skills, but beyond that we have to work out our own solutions to our own predicaments. More and more, over the years, my own teaching has focused on helping people to do just that – in effect, to learn for themselves.

In the same way, I believe, we shall increasingly see a distinction between 'business studies', being the stock of common understanding, and 'management learning', the art of helping individuals and organizations to shape their own futures and to make the most of their own assets. Different institutions will concentrate on one or the other, recognizing that they may be connected but are not the same. It was always wrong to think that they were.

THIRTY-ONE

◆

THE NEW AGE OF POSITIVE POWER

'Things fall apart, the centre cannot hold' – Yeats' words, so often quoted, so often true. These past weeks I have been in Italy, watching that fascinating country worry lest it fall apart. There is no political centre in Italy any more. They talk of the 'ghost in the polling booth', meaning the missing centre which so many would like to vote for, were it to exist.

No political centre, maybe, but there is a massive administrative centre. In Italy you need a licence for everything and the patience to wait for it. Even the University of Bologna, which has been going strong since 1300, cannot create a new course without the approval of the Ministry in Rome, while permission to restore your house can take years, and reams of official forms. But if you hope for new initiatives, or even new ideas, from this bureaucracy, you hope in vain.

Here, then, is the supreme irony – a centre which controls everything but does nothing, a centre with all the formal power but without the leadership to use it positively. It is a recipe for unlimited 'negative power' and an invitation to corruption. It is not, unfortunately, a phenomenon peculiar to Italy. Negative power haunts the corridors of every large organization.

If you don't have the authority to make something happen – positive power – you will almost certainly have the means to stop it happening – negative power. 'I'm sorry, but the form has been incorrectly completed and the last day for submitting it has now passed.'

Big centres, therefore, with their proliferating bureaucracies, often stifle movement. Energy comes from power, but without the power to make changes, to create and to initiate, the only energy around comes from negative power. Politics and corruption abound in such places. It is tempting, after all, to be paid for not working, for not exercising the power which you could. All power corrupts, but negative power corrupts more insidiously.

The answer to all this is easy to give, but hard to implement. Shrink the centre. It should be stronger but smaller, offering more leadership and fewer licences, concentrating on 'where to?' and 'what for?' not 'how?' If ABB can oversee 225,000 people with 120 in the Zurich centre; if Boots can do it with less than 100 in theirs; and Mars, reputedly, with less than 20, large centres will soon be a thing of the past. Small centres, it seems, concentrate the mind wonderfully, leave no time or people for unnecessary double-checking, and force one to give positive power to those lower down and farther out. Where there is positive power, there is no need to activate one's negative power.

Small centres work on the assumption that if you get the big decisions right the little ones will take care of themselves. Even if the small ones sometimes go wrong, the energy released by all the positive power around will more than make up for the odd error of judgment. Besides, it is much cheaper that way, because trust costs less than licences. Small centres rely on trust; trust that the others are competent, trust that they will act in the best interests of the organization. Trust, however, means having the right people to begin with, training them right, treating them right, knowing them well and talking with them constantly. Organizations with small centres must be fanatical about selection, training and communication – all the soft skills of the new organizations.

It can be lonely, however, in these small centres. As a vice-president of ABB told me once: 'All we can do is to watch the herd, and observe, with some relief, that in general it is heading in the right direction!' If some cattle are seen to be straying, the alarm bells ring in this sort of organization and a ranger is sent out to rein them in. But if the herd is going where it should, then it is left to get on with it. The controls are quick and focused but they look at the ends not the means; the results, not the processes.

Poor Italy, therefore, which has lived so long with a culture of negative power. No matter who the leader, it is hard to change such a culture. Where one has long been rewarded or promoted not for success but for absence of errors, it is hard to change one's outlook. In the places of negative power, positive power is not always welcomed. Licences are easier to produce than new initiatives.

For the rest of us, it should be easier. Our centres are smaller and getting smaller. There is more of a liking for individual responsibility, and, I hope, less relish in saying 'no'. As more people taste the pleasures of an organization built on the principles of positive power, this way of arranging things is becoming more fashionable. We used to design organizations to prevent people from making mistakes. We now try to design them to help people make a positive difference. Fashion often seems more powerful than any theory. Here, for once, fashion and theory are walking hand in hand.

THIRTY-TWO

◆

ALL CHANGE IN THE WORLD OF WORK

Perhaps we all need an earthquake to remind us that we should take nothing for granted, not even the ground we stand on. We should certainly not rely on the rules of economics, or of work, remaining constant. These days, some of the things which we have always taken for granted are looking less sure. Productivity, for example, is turning out to be a two-edged weapon. We need, as we all know, to get more productive in all our enterprises in order to stay competitive and to grow more wealth. That was fine as long as the productivity improved in line with the growth rate. The new growth then sucked in the jobs which the improved productivity displaced.

Nowadays, however, competition requires our productivity to improve at something like 5 to 10% per annum. No developed country can sustain overall growth rates that high. We are, inevitably, getting rid of more jobs than we can replace, yet if we don't improve our productivity that fast, we will lose even more jobs when whole enterprises close down. It gets worse. It used to be that government and the public services, what one might call the non-competitive sector, was a reliable source of jobs, unhindered by too much insistence on productivity because the output couldn't really be measured. Now, however, we have re-competitioned government, turning everything – schools, hospitals, government agencies, even the prisons – into independent enterprises, judged by the way they turn their inputs into outputs, just like any business. They too are now in the grip of that inexorable formula $-\frac{1}{2} \times 2 \times 3 = P$, half as many people, paid twice as well, producing three times as much.

That formula works fine, maybe, for the half that stays, but not for the other half. That's where the old ideas about work are no longer working. There aren't proper jobs out there any more, but there are customers, potential customers, if we can work out what they want and deliver it.

There is work out there if we were able to turn ourselves into tiny independent businesses – 'portfolio people' I call them, with a portfolio of clients and products. The trouble is that we prepared ourselves for a world of jobs not customers. As independents, we don't know what to sell or how to sell it, even how to price it or make out an invoice. We shall have to learn.

Part of the trouble is the changing nature of the source of wealth, of property. Forget land, buildings or machines – the real source of wealth today is intelligence, applied intelligence. We talk glibly of 'intellectual property' without taking on board what it really means. It isn't just patent rights and brand names, it is the brains of the place. When the market values a business at three or four times the value of its tangible assets, it is the market's best guess at the added value of the 'intelligence quotient' of the organization.

But intelligence does not behave like any other sort of property. Government cannot hand it out by decree. You can't even give it to someone unless they already have some.

And if you do give it to someone, you still keep it. Odd. Intelligence, in short, tends to go where intelligence is, in the short term at least. If, therefore, intelligence does become established as the new source of wealth, society will become increasingly lumpy, with lumps of the rich and bigger lumps of those without any of this new property at all. There won't be a property-owning democracy if only 30% get an education beyond 18, in a world where it will need to be 70% to cope with the work on offer. We are still a down-skilled society in an up-skilled world.

Intelligence as property brings other challenges to businesses. If your real assets are truly your intelligent people, the ones who create and maintain your intellectual property, then those people are precious. Unlike other assets, however, they can walk out of the door. To stop them walking we shall have to make them quasi-partners in the enterprise, with large bonus schemes, share schemes and, I suspect, some of the rights of ownership. Equity investment is going to get even more risky, when you are, in effect, betting on other people's brains, and increased risk will want increased and shorter-term rewards. In the short-term life is going to get more difficult. In the end, in order to protect the business from impatient investors, we may have to reform company law, putting limits on the powers of the financiers.

Earthquakes last 45 seconds. This economic earthquake may last 45 years, but unfortunately we are right in the middle of it. The middle of an earthquake is not the best time to start re-doing the foundations, but we have no choice. It's either a major rethink about the new types of work and property, and all their implications, or waking up in the morning to a scene of desolation.

THIRTY-THREE

◆

THE GUN LAWS OF GALAPAGOS

As you approach the security check at Logan Airport in Boston, a large notice advises you that 'All guns must be declared.' My first thought was to worry about the efficiency of the security – why couldn't the apparatus detect the guns itself? – but then I went on to worry about a society which prohibits smoking in most public places, but allows citizens to carry guns wheresoever they want.

The right of self-defence, and to carry arms for that purpose, is, of course, a fundamental part of the American tradition. There is, however, another side to that tradition – namely, the responsibility to look after oneself.

It is that responsibility for one's own life and destiny which is worrying more and more Americans as they find themselves thrown back on their own resources. For as long as most middle-income Americans can remember, a work organization of some sort has been theirs, providing them with that middle income, with the promise that it would continue and come accompanied with the insurance to pay their healthcare costs. For those who could only aspire to that income and status, the dream was there – there was a ladder waiting for anyone with the gumption to climb it. For everyone there was, potentially, a house in the suburbs, two kids, two cars and, if they wanted, two guns.

No longer. In spite of a fast-reviving economy, the American dream now looks more like a fantasy for many. You need two incomes now to live as well as your parents did on one. As organizations shrink back to their cores and concentrate on short-term survival, they no longer offer any sort of permanent home.

The middle-income managers are feeling the pain for the first time. It is even worse below them, because the ladder of opportunity, which beckoned so many to America, is now broken above the first rung. In the past, the organization was the starting point, the place where one trained for work and learnt to work. Now you have to do it outside, as a personal entrepreneur, with total responsibility for one's own training, development and, of course, income. People were not prepared for this. Many cannot cope.

America is busier than it was two years ago. But the tension and the stress is also higher. It is becoming a land of fat cats and scavengers, but the fat cats worry that it may not last and the scavengers scurry to survive. The kinder, gentler America which was once promised seems further away than ever.

A recent article in *Inc* magazine was entitled 'It's not the same America' and listed the obstacles to getting started in work today, now that the start has, so often, got to be as an independent. The obstacles included excessive regulation of small and new businesses, regulated monopolies, restricted access to initial capital, a welfare trap which discourages both savings and initiatives and, most crucially, a public education system that spews out so-called students unprepared for the baffling world ahead.

As the economic system has grown more complex, it has also grown more Darwinian. The highly skilled prosper; the skilled survive, and the unskilled are the victims. As Darwin pointed out, the species will adapt to survive, but it takes generations. Many become extinct in the process.

It is easy to say that we should do something about all those obstacles and the independent life that faces so many of us. But that will cost money, time and effort – things that won't be forthcoming without a change of heart and mind. As long as it is each to ourselves, as long as success and self-esteem is measured by the scorecard of materialism, so long will it be a selfish, uncaring and shortsighted world. It is shortsighted because in the end we shoot ourselves in the foot, turning those who could have been our customers into our dependants, and we, who could have been their benefactors, into their victims. It is, I am sure, no coincidence that a recent survey revealed that 70% of crimes of robbery and violence are committed by the unemployed, taking vengeance on the rich.

It is also, I hope, no coincidence that a new book is riding high on the bestseller list in America. It is *The Spirit of Community* by Amitni Etzioni. It is a call for a sense of community to be revived in our societies, to balance the instinctive individuality that seems to have run amok. The book must be striking a chord. Not, I suspect, because 'community' – a rather weasel word – is the perfect answer, but because so many believe that there must be more to life, and indeed to business, than mere money, or more money; that success can and should be measured in other ways; and that there is, after all, such a thing as 'society'.

If all responsibility means is the right to carry your own gun, we shall all get shot. Maybe, this time round, we in Britain can show America a glimpse of the future.

THIRTY-FOUR

◆

LIVING FAST, DYING RICH

How fast do you walk? The urban Japanese move fastest, followed by the Americans, English, Taiwanese and Italians. The Indonesians move the slowest of all. This intriguing fact comes from an important new book, *After the Gold Rush*, by Stewart Lansley and the Henley Centre (Century, £20). The message is clear. The richer you are, it seems, the faster you live.

You not only walk faster, you also work longer, strive harder and suffer more stress in order to become richer, or perhaps just to survive in a modern society. Over the last 20 years, working hours have gone up, in the US, by the equivalent of one extra month a year; commuting time is up by 23 hours a year, and vacation time down by three-and-a-half days. That's nothing compared with the Japanese who now work 400 hours a year more than most Europeans (equivalent to an extra ten weeks) and take only 7.9 days a year of paid holiday. Not much time, there, for spending all those extra riches.

No wonder, then, that the Japanese have a word – *karoshi* – to describe death from overwork, or that half of them, apparently, live in fear of such a death. Even in more sleepy Britain, Professor Cary Cooper has found that half of the company chairmen and chief executives in one of his surveys suffered from hours-related stress. For more ordinary mortals it is depression or the simple inability to cope which takes over after a while – not so much *karoshi* as 'can't take it'. A study last year by the Massachusetts Institute of Technology reckoned that depression at work was costing the country $47bn, much the same as heart disease. The difference was that the costs of heart disease were paid by the patients and their insurers, whereas most of the costs of depression were invisible and fell on the organization.

What are we doing to ourselves? Is it all part of the new competitiveness, what we have to do in order to survive, both as individuals in the firm and as the firm in the market? Or are we creating a new myth for ourselves, a new ideal, the consumed executive as the modern hero? Either way it bodes ill for our society if the best and brightest end up having no time for anything or anyone but themselves and their work, and if the price of success has to be total immersion in that work.

One suspects that it does not do the work much good either, after a certain point. Even without falling prey to depression, 80-hour weeks are no better for senior executives than they are for junior doctors. Both can make false diagnoses and wrong prescriptions when suffering from extreme weariness.

The symptoms of tired behaviour are well established; it isn't the bleary eyes or the dropping jaw, it is the imperative to make things simpler in order to operate. We do this by polarizing issues into black and white, right or wrong, no greys or in-betweens; we do it by stereotyping people and situations to fit them into familiar boxes which we know how to deal with; we shorten the time horizons and postpone all the difficult decisions until another day. When tired, we also talk rather than listen – it helps to keep us awake; we also let emotion rather than reason come to the fore, and to keep us going we look to drink and other stimulants.

The tactics work – for us. It is the organization, the customers or the clients and those around us who suffer from the unintended consequences of our simplifications. Those around us, in their turn, start to emulate the hours and, often, the behaviours of those above them. Work then becomes addictive for us all. The problems of the workplace are, besides, often easier to deal with than the problems and decisions of the world outside.

We do need that adrenalin. We need our deadlines, targets and the pressure to deliver. Without them I, person-ally, find that I sink into lethargy and self-doubt. It is, as ever, a question of balance or, more accurately, of a compensating opposite. Were there is stress, let there also be times and places of tranquillity, what Alvin Toffler once called stability zones. Where there is a need for focus, for concentration on the immediate and the detailed, let it be followed by a chance to walk in other worlds, to look beyond our work, to meet with people who know not what we do. 'I am happy for you that your work is going so well,' my wife said to me once, when I was working those 80-hour weeks. 'I just think you should know that you have become the most boring man I know.'

It would be a sad consequence of all our achievements and of economic progress if we had no time to enjoy what we had wrought or if, at the end of our days we could only agree with the preacher in the Book of Ecclesiastes who lamented that he 'looked on all the labour that I had laboured to do, and behold, all was vanity and a striving after wind.'

THIRTY-FIVE

◆

HOW DO YOU MANAGE WHEN YOU CAN'T SEE THE PEOPLE?

I found myself recently at a conference of librarians – all 800 of them. It was not the sort of occasion where you would expect to get a sudden glimpse of the future, but that was what happened. The chairman started by reminding us of the long and dignified tradition of the library, and of the importance of the librarian as the guardian of its treasures and its facilities. Change, however, was at the door. The computer terminal was replacing the shelves. It's true. Where I used to go to wooden trays and cards to find a book in the library at my business school, I now go to a terminal; and if I want a copy of an article I no longer take the journal to a photocopier, I print it straight from the screen.

Actually, said an editor at that conference, we are considering whether we ought not to stop printing and distributing our journal and instead insert it directly into the data bases of the libraries. 'Why then,' said someone else, 'I need not go near the library, I could read it off the screen in my own home.' I watched the faces of the librarians then, as they took in the implications of what had been said. They were contemplating the strange reality of a 'virtual library' – a library without a library, a concept not a place.

We are all beginning to see more signs of these 'virtual organizations', organizations which do not need to have all the people, or sometimes any of the people, in one place in order to deliver their service. The organization exists but you can't see it. It is a network not an office. As technology continues to turn the unlikely into the familiar, it becomes cheaper and quicker to communicate with people electronically and telephonically rather than face to face in a room. Offices are expensive. So is time spent in travelling to them. If you can do without them it is cheaper. If you go into an organization, these days, the odds are that half of the offices are empty. Their occupants are not truanting, they are 'out working', in car, train or plane, at home or at their customers' premises. Why keep an office which is empty half the time?

But then you have to manage people whom you do not see. Chiat-Day, the Los Angeles based advertising agency, is a business which actually calls itself a virtual office. 'Work,' says Laurie Coots, the Senior VP in charge of Administration and Business Development, is, 'something you do, not somewhere you go to.' People work wherever it suits them, going in to what I once described as the 'clubhouse' or minimalist office only for essential meetings. Chiat-Day has to trust that its people are doing what they ought to be doing because there is no way that they can check up on them when they are out of sight.

The trust is the rub. Virtual organizations are built on trust. This should be good news, because it is both cheaper and more pleasing to trust people than to regulate, inspect and control them. But you can't trust someone you do not know, you can't trust someone who is not committed to the goals of the organization, and you can't trust someone who lets you down. Obvious maybe, but the implications are important.

1. The choice of people becomes more important than ever. One bad apple ruins the batch. Recruitment, placement and promotion become key managerial priorities. An interview may no longer be enough. I suspect that we shall see more probationary contracts to give people time to be sure.

2. How many people can you know well enough to trust? Probably not more than 50 at most. Organization units must become smaller and more stable so that people can get to know each other over time. Teams are now the fashion, but for teams to stay together the teams have to be flexible enough to tackle a range of tasks. Trust, therefore, leads to a demand for constant updating and re-education.

3. Trust is fuelled by talk. E-mail, voice-mail and every other sort of mail are essential if out of sight is not going to mean out of mind. But hi-tech needs to be balanced by hi-touch. Video conferences work better when the participants are friends not strangers. Virtual organizations make a point of meeting together, not necessarily in offices or in office time, so that they can know each other personally as well as electronically.

4. The vision and values stuff really matters. If there is no common goal people put their own goals first. If, however, those who are out of sight think that they are only working to make some anonymous shareholders a bit richer, they are unlikely to do more than they need to. There has to be more point to their work than that, and many of the hi-touch meetings of the group will be concerned to re-enforce the mission and goals of the organization, in order to win the commitment of its people.

5. Trust is tough. If people let you down you cannot afford to trust them any more. Virtual organizations require loyalty and good performance. They reward results but they have to punish incompetence and repeated failure. If they don't, they will have to re-institute inspections and controls. Do not expect a guaranteed job for life from an organization based on trust. The security has to be earned.

Like it or not, the times are changing. More of us are going to have to run organizations which we cannot see, and learn the ways to do it.

CHARLES HANDY

THE EMPTY RAINCOAT

Charles Handy

'Life will never be easy, or sure, or perfect. Best understood backwards, we have to live it forwards – with all its contradictions. There is a paradox at the heart of things. The challenge of the future is to find a pathway through the paradoxes.'

* Are you on the way to Davy's Bar?
* When is the moment to take the Sigmoid Curve?
* Do you know the Doughnut Principle?
* What is a Chinese contract?

The changes which Charles Handy, Britain's foremost business guru, foresaw in *The Age of Unreason* are happening. Endless growth can create a candyfloss economy, and capitalism must be its own sternest critic.

Charles Handy reaches here for a philosophy beyond the mechanics of business organisations, beyond material choices, to try to establish an alternative universe, where life and work are re-grounded in a natural sense of continuity, connection and purposeful direction.

£7.99
Arrow Business Books
ISBN 0 09 930125 3

THE GODS OF MANAGEMENT

Charles Handy

The four gods of the title symbolise the very different styles of management and culture to be found in today's organisations. Zeus is the dynamic entrepreneur who rules over companies of the **club culture**, characterised by speed of decision and rapid, intuitive communication. Apollo, god of order and bureaucracy, is the patron of the **role culture,** based not on personalities but on definition of the jobs to be done. Athena, goddess of craftsmen, recognises only expertise as the basis of power and influence: hers is the **task culture.** Dionysus is the god preferred by artists and professionals within the **existential culture**, people who owe little or no allegiance to a boss.

Under the witty and sparkling allegory Charles Handy, Britain's foremost business guru, makes a serious analysis of the changing patterns of work and business. Management is not a precise science but has aspects of a creative and political process which is influenced by the prevailing culture and traditions of the organisation. His theme is illustrated with a wealth of case studies and examples drawn from business around the world.

This book is a world bestseller which is required reading for managers, business students and everyone who wants to be a survivor in a world of constantly changing organisational culture.

£7.99
Arrow Business Books
ISBN 0 09 954841 0